Betty Crocker's
Dinner for Two

Director of Photography: JOHN GARETTI

GOLDEN PRESS / NEW YORK
Western Publishing Company, Inc.
Racine, Wisconsin

W9-BDD-227

REVISED EDITION
with recipes selected from the original edition
First Printing This Edition, 1980

Copyright © 1977, 1973 by General Mills, Inc., Minneapolis, Minnesota.
All rights reserved. No portion of this book may be reprinted or reproduced
in any form or any manner without the written permission of the publishers,
except by a reviewer who wishes to quote brief passages in connection with a review.
Printed in the U.S.A. by Western Publishing Company, Inc.
Published by Golden Press, New York, New York.
Library of Congress Catalog Card Number: 72-90756
Golden® and Golden Press® are trademarks of
Western Publishing Company, Inc.

Contents

when minutes matter

Easy dinners that let you shortcut—
without being shortchanged

more dimes than dollars

Inventive dinners that make
the most of a little money

EVERYDAY FAVORITES

Dinners that make tried-and-true
seem suddenly new

Planning Ahead

Dinners that star a "big" meat buy—with repeat
performances as sparkling as First Night

TWO IS COMPANY

Memory-making dinners that
say, "Tonight is special"

Basic Know-How

Just-for-two tips on shopping,
storing and kitchen coping

What's So Special About Cooking For Two?

Two is a very good number. Or so the songwriters say. The joys of being a twosome have been catalogued in enough lyrics to reach the moon (in June) and back again. But somehow, very few of the choruses praise the pleasures of cooking for two.

Could it be because it's considered more of a problem than a pleasure? If so, this book will surely help dispel that notion. Not that the shopping, planning and preparation involved are all fun and games. But there are some very definite advantages to setting two places (or even one) which you may not have given much thought to before.

Cheer for Your Choices

The advantages of cooking for few...what are they? "Choice" is the word that almost says it all. Think about it a bit. When you cook small, you're more apt to allow yourself the out-of-season fruit or out-of-reach meat—a choice you'd never consider if you were cooking for more. And you can take full advantage of the wealth of frozen, prepared and packaged foods that are especially geared to ones and twos.

Then there's the matter of mood. More choices! Pairs or singles needn't be confined to same-place dining. If you don't feel like setting your every-night table, go where the spirit moves you. You can "tray" it in the living room for a TV special, play it cool outdoors on a stuffy night or be casual as you please at the kitchen counter.

Plotting the Plan

The twosome does have special problems, it's true. But chin up—this book will show you how to tackle them. To begin with, there's the matter of marketing. A major dither for anyone, but particularly so for doubles or singles. But all the recipes in this book are just the right size, so you'll know exactly how much to buy. To take you one step further, the bulk of the "Basic Know-How" chapter is devoted to helping you shop wisely. You'll find solutions for other problem posers, too. There are complete meal plans for rush times, for tight-money times, for urge-to-splurge times. All just for two. But that doesn't mean you have to think small. The "Planning Ahead" chapter actually encourages you to think big—to take advantage of the economies and pleasures of family-size roasts and the variety that can come from their leftovers.

What's more, every single recipe and every menu has been tested in the Betty Crocker Kitchens and by twosomes all across the country. So we know they'll work for you.

Once you've tried these menus "by the book," feel free to improvise—to put new lyrics to the music. Switch vegetables, swap salads, ring in a different entrée. For a heartier meal, add rolls or biscuits; for a lighter one, ease up on dessert. And many "bonus" main dishes have been included in each chapter to menu-mix as you please.

The Balancing Act

So you make your menu by putting your favorites together, right? Not quite. Good nutrition counts, too. And heavily. The menus in the book were planned with an eye to nutritional balance, so you're bound to pick up a tip or two. And you can do the same on your own by keeping the "Basic Four" guidelines in mind.

But remember dinner is only one of your meals. You need to be clued in as to what else is (or was) on the eating program for the rest of the day to do the planning job properly. Dinner can plug in some of the gaps, but it shouldn't be expected to carry more than a third of the daily load.

Contrast Is the Key

Anything else? Just a few more ground rules—and they can be summed up in a simple phrase: Think contrast.

Think contrast in color. A white fish with a bright vegetable, a pale slaw with a ring of green pepper, chocolate pudding with a jolt of snowy topping. When you plan the kinds of foods you serve, try to imagine how they'll look on the plate.

Think contrast in texture. Put something soft with something crisp. Pair something chewy with something smooth.

Think contrast in flavor. Spice is nice, but cool it with something mild. All bland makes a dull meal, and all tart isn't smart.

The "Basic Four"
YOU NEED THESE EVERY DAY

1 Meats	**2** Vegetables and Fruits	**3** Milk	**4** Breads and Cereals
2 or more servings (also includes poultry, fish, eggs, dried beans or peas and peanut butter)	4 or more servings (plan on one dark green or yellow vegetable every other day and one citrus fruit daily)	2 or more cups (also includes cheese and ice cream)	4 or more servings (whole grain, enriched, restored or fortified)

Remember to include sweets, fats and extra servings from the basic four groups to help round out meals and provide additional food energy and food values.

Rarely would you care to repeat one food in the same meal, such as Waldorf salad and apple pie (even if apples *are* the best buy of the week).

Think contrast in temperature. Sultry day or not, one hot dish gives a meal more appeal. By the same token, an ice-cream dessert refreshes even on a frosty night.

Think contrast in shapes and sizes. This one is relatively easy. An example: If you're serving hamburger patties, carrots and potatoes, cut the carrots into sticks instead of rounds, and perhaps serve French fried or au gratin potatoes instead of little potato balls.

How's Your Timing?

Let's assume you've decided on a menu that rates an A in nutrition and appeal. What happens next makes the difference between calm and chaos. Scheduling enters the scene. Look over the timing hints given with many of the menus—particularly, and quite naturally, in the chapter called "When Minutes Matter." You'll realize that successful timing is more than a matter of instinct and luck. It's part common sense, part experience and part plain confidence. Common sense tells you, for instance, that you're plotting a collision course if everything requires last-minute attention. Basically, the more you can fix ahead (the night before, morning before or even an hour before), the easier it will be as "curtain time" approaches.

To avoid the pitfalls of sorry scheduling, jot down all the foods you plan to serve, then note the time you estimate it will take you to prepare and cook each one. Obviously, you'll start with the longest and work your way to the speediest. It's that simple.

Rely on cook-and-serve ware and any labor-saving appliances you may have to help speed things along. And if someone shares the just-before-you-serve jobs, you really have it made.

Flair—The Extra Dimension

You don't need an extensive (or expensive) wardrobe of linens, dishes and accessories to add flair to your table. Not at all. Chances are you already have everything it takes to add a special touch right at your fingertips. Simple things like a basket heaped with glossy lemons and limes, seashells piled in a wooden bowl, a small green plant, a coffee mug filled with daisies. Inexpensive place mats and napkins serve a practical purpose and add zing to your table.

And don't forget decorative garnishes… those unexpected little flicks of color and flavor that add an exclamation point to an everyday plate. Parsley was born to be the universal trim, but don't stop there. Try a sprig of mint, a few celery leaves or a pickle slice. Such simple ways to "style up" a dish.

Flair is letting the "creative you" be free to find beauty and surprise all around.

Now, read on. Use the ideas and recipes that follow as your starting point. Then add your own special touches, play up your own preferences. Discover the continuing adventure and reward in every "dinner for two" you share. Whether you are recently wed, apartment-sharers or a career couple … whether you are back to two … whether you are alone and on your own … you'll find that this book is the one for you.

when minutes matter

Easy dinners that let you shortcut—without being shortchanged

What does it say about you if dinner takes but 20 minutes from in-the-door to at-the-table? It says that you're an advance planner, just waiting for countdown. First, on with the water (for the noodles and frozen asparagus), next to the stroganoff and finally the salad. The dessert's in the freezer; the meringue top browns while instant coffee brews.

Steak Stroganoff
Parsleyed Noodles
Buttered Asparagus Spears
Herbed Tomatoes
Individual Brownie Alaskas

STEAK STROGANOFF

1 medium onion, thinly sliced
1 tablespoon salad oil
2 beef cubed steaks
2 tablespoons flour
2 tablespoons salad oil
½ teaspoon salt
¼ cup dairy sour cream
1 can (2 ounces) mushroom stems and pieces

In 8-inch skillet, cook and stir onion in 1 tablespoon oil until tender, about 4 minutes. Remove from skillet and set aside.

Coat steaks with flour. Heat 2 tablespoons oil in same skillet; cook steaks over medium heat, about 4 minutes on each side. Sprinkle with salt. Place steaks on warm platter or dinner plates.

Drain fat from skillet. Add onion, sour cream and mushrooms (with liquid) to skillet; heat, stirring occasionally. Serve sauce on steaks.

2 servings.

PARSLEYED NOODLES

Cook 4 ounces noodles (about 1½ cups) in 1 quart boiling salted water (2 teaspoons salt) until tender, about 7 minutes. Drain noodles and return to saucepan. Add 1 tablespoon butter or margarine and 1 teaspoon parsley flakes and toss.

2 servings.

HERBED TOMATOES

1 medium or 2 small tomatoes, cut into slices
  Crisp salad greens
2 tablespoons oil-and-vinegar dressing
  Salt and pepper
¼ teaspoon freeze-dried chives
  Dash thyme

Arrange tomato slices on salad greens. Drizzle dressing on tomatoes. Sprinkle with salt, pepper, chives and thyme.

2 servings.

INDIVIDUAL BROWNIE ALASKAS

2 unfrosted brownies or date bars, 3x3 inches, or commercially prepared sponge shortcakes
  Vanilla, coffee or peppermint ice cream
1 egg white
2 tablespoons sugar

Place brownies on ungreased baking sheet. Top each with scoop or slice of ice cream; place in freezer while preparing meringue. (Ice cream must be very hard before covering with meringue.)

Heat oven to 450°. Beat egg white until foamy. Beat in sugar gradually; continue beating until stiff and glossy. Do not underbeat. Quickly spread meringue on ice cream *and sides of brownies,* being careful to seal meringue to baking sheet. Bake until light brown, about 3 minutes. Place in freezer (up to 24 hours) or serve immediately.

2 servings.

Taco time—in no time. Packaged shells and help-yourself fillings make easy work of this dinner with a Latin beat. Ground beef, shredded lettuce, cheese and tomatoes are the stuffers in the picture on page 7. Want an extra measure of heartiness? Canned refried beans do the job quickly.

TACOS

½ pound ground beef
1 can (8 ounces) tomato sauce
2 tablespoons instant minced onion
½ teaspoon garlic salt
¼ teaspoon chili powder
  Dash pepper
4 or 5 taco shells
½ to ¾ cup shredded lettuce
½ cup shredded natural Cheddar
  cheese
½ cup chopped tomato, if desired
  Hot Sauce (below) or bottled
  taco sauce

In 8-inch skillet, cook and stir meat until brown. Drain off fat. Stir in tomato sauce, onion, garlic salt, chili powder and pepper. Simmer uncovered 15 minutes.

While meat mixture simmers, heat taco shells as directed on package. Fill taco shells with meat mixture. Top each with lettuce, cheese and chopped tomato. Serve with Hot Sauce.

4 or 5 tacos.

Hot Sauce

Mix ⅓ cup chili sauce and ¼ teaspoon red pepper sauce or 1 teaspoon minced hot chili pepper.

Note: Shredded Swiss or mozzarella cheese can be substituted for the Cheddar cheese. And for variety, when filling the taco shells, add one of the following: ¼ cup chopped avocado, ¼ cup chopped olives, ¼ cup chopped onion or ¼ cup chopped green pepper.

FRUIT WITH QUICK CUSTARD SAUCE

1 orange, pared and sectioned,
  or 1 can (11 ounces) mandarin
  orange segments, drained
1 banana
¼ cup canned vanilla pudding
2 tablespoons milk

Divide orange sections between dessert dishes. Slice banana into dishes. Mix pudding and milk; spoon onto fruits.

2 servings.

Variations

Pineapple with Quick Custard Sauce: Substitute 1 can (13½ ounces) pineapple chunks, drained and chilled, for the orange and banana. Top each serving with ½ teaspoon strawberry jelly.

Berries with Quick Custard Sauce: Substitute 1 cup strawberry halves, raspberries or blueberries for the orange and banana.

Something to Know About...

Cut off the peel and white membrane of the orange. Then cut along both sides of each dividing membrane until you reach the core and can lift out the orange section.

Tacos
Refried Beans
Fruit with Quick Custard Sauce

Quick Cheese Fondue
Crisp Green Salad
Fresh Fruit

QUICK CHEESE FONDUE

1 can (11 ounces) condensed
   Cheddar cheese soup
1 cup shredded Cheddar, Swiss or
   Parmesan cheese (about 4
   ounces)
2 green onions, finely chopped
⅛ teaspoon garlic powder
   Dash red pepper sauce
   Dippers (right)

In fondue pot, saucepan or chafing dish, heat soup and cheese over medium heat, stirring occasionally, until cheese is melted. Stir in onion, garlic powder and red pepper sauce. Serve with three or more of the Dippers, cut into bite-size pieces if necessary. If fondue becomes too thick, stir in small amount apple juice, white wine or beer.

2 servings.

Dippers

Croutons
French bread
White or rye hard rolls
Toast sticks
Dried beef rolls
Cooked chicken or turkey
Frankfurters
Cooked ham
Luncheon meat
Cooked shrimp
Cooked asparagus (crisp-tender)
Cooked broccoli (crisp-tender)
Cooked Brussels sprouts (crisp-tender)
Cauliflower
Celery
Stuffed olives
Green onions
Green peppers
Cherry tomatoes

The trick here is in the timing—the way you cleverly juggle burgers, noodles and rolls so everything crosses the finish line together. It all works out so that dinner's ready in an unhassled 30 minutes. Timetable: Mix and shape burgers; start noodles. About 10 minutes before sit-down, begin broiling meat and simmering noodles with sauce. When the patties are turned, add split rolls. Pretty up the plates with a garnish of tomato wedges and parsley or celery leaves.

PINEAPPLE BURGERS

½ pound ground beef
½ teaspoon salt
2 canned pineapple slices,
   well drained*
2 tablespoons brown sugar
2 tablespoons catsup
2 teaspoons prepared mustard

Set oven control at broil and/or 550°. Shape meat into 4 thin patties; sprinkle with salt. Place pineapple slice on each of 2 patties. Top with remaining patties and press edges together to seal.

Place patties on rack in broiler pan. Broil with tops 4 inches from heat until brown, 3 to 5 minutes. Mix brown sugar, catsup and mustard. Turn patties; spoon brown sugar mixture on patties and broil until of desired doneness, 3 to 5 minutes.

2 servings.

*Extra pineapple slices? Serve as fruit for tomorrow's breakfast. Or use in Broiled Ham and Sweet Potatoes (page 17) or Tomato-Pineapple Salad (page 20).

NOODLES ALMONDINE

Measure contents of 1 package (5.5 ounces) noodles almondine; divide in half (approximately 1 cup noodles and 3 rounded tablespoons Sauce Mix).* Cook half the noodles in 3 cups boiling salted water until tender, 7 to 8 minutes. Drain noodles and return to saucepan.

Stir in half the Sauce Mix and half the amounts of butter and milk called for on package. Sprinkle half the Almonds on top.

2 servings.

*To store remaining mix, close package securely; use within 2 weeks. Serve Noodles Almondine with ham, salmon, veal cutlets, chicken or hamburgers.

HERBED CRUSTY ROLLS

Set oven control at broil and/or 550°. Split 2 hard rolls horizontally. Spread soft butter or margarine on halves and sprinkle with Italian herb seasoning. Place on rack in broiler pan. Broil with tops 4 inches from heat until golden brown, about 4 minutes.

2 servings.

CHOCOLATE-PEANUT BUTTER SUNDAES

Mix 2 tablespoons peanut butter and ¼ cup chocolate syrup until smooth. Serve on scoops of vanilla ice cream.

2 servings.

Variations

Honey-Peanut Butter Sundaes: Substitute ¼ cup honey for the chocolate syrup.

Hot Chocolate-Mocha Sundaes: Omit peanut butter; heat chocolate syrup with ¼ teaspoon powdered instant coffee.

Pineapple Burgers
Noodles Almondine
**Lettuce Wedges
with Favorite Dressing**
Herbed Crusty Rolls
**Chocolate-Peanut Butter
Sundaes**

LIVER ITALIANO

2 tablespoons flour
½ teaspoon garlic salt
½ pound sliced beef liver,
   cut into 1-inch pieces
1 tablespoon salad oil
1 can (8 ounces) tomato sauce
1 green pepper, cut into thin
   strips
1 small onion, thinly sliced and
   separated into rings
3 to 4 ounces uncooked spaghetti
2 tablespoons grated Parmesan
   cheese

Mix flour and garlic salt; coat meat with flour mixture. Heat oil in 8-inch skillet; brown meat over medium heat. Stir in tomato sauce; add green pepper and onion. Cover and simmer until done, 8 to 10 minutes.

While meat simmers, cook spaghetti as directed on package. Serve meat mixture on spaghetti and sprinkle cheese on top.

2 servings.

Something to Know About...

"Liver's good for you!" Sound familiar? Well, it's no old wives' tale. Liver is positively packed with essential nutrients, including protein, iron, vitamin A, riboflavin and niacin. It's a good idea to work it into your meal plan every week or two. But liver is more perishable than other meats; unless it's frozen, it should be used within 2 days after purchase.

Beef and pork liver are frequently braised or fried and are sometimes ground for loaves and patties. Baby beef, veal (calf) and lamb liver are usually panfried, broiled or pan-broiled. Before cooking, peel or trim any membrane from the liver if necessary. If you simply can't take it "straight," try grinding it up as part of your meat loaf mixture or use it as a sandwich spread.

GREEN BEAN TOSSED SALAD

1 can (8 ounces) cut green beans,
   chilled
1 can (2 ounces) mushroom stems
   and pieces, chilled
1 cup bite-size pieces lettuce
1 teaspoon chopped pimiento
3 tablespoons Italian dressing
2 lettuce cups

Drain green beans and mushrooms. Toss beans, mushrooms, lettuce, pimiento and dressing in bowl. Divide salad between lettuce cups.

2 servings.

LIME FRAPPÉ

2 cups crushed ice
½ can (6-ounce size) frozen
   limeade concentrate (about
   ¼ cup)*
2 tablespoons sugar
1 drop green food color

In blender, mix all ingredients on medium speed until mixture is consistency of sherbet. (Scrape sides once or twice if necessary.) Serve immediately or store in freezer until serving time.

2 servings.

Note: To crush ice, use an ice crusher or wrap 9 or 10 ice cubes in towel and crush with mallet or hammer.

*Leftover limeade concentrate? To the rescue for tomorrow's dessert: Top servings of cut-up fresh or canned fruit with spoonfuls of the partially thawed concentrate.

Two head starts are better than one. So buy the pork chops smoked (which quickens cooking time). And pick the salad that best fits your schedule. Depending on which end of the day you have a time bind, make the Sauerkraut Salad early in the morning or even the night before (the longer the flavors blend, the tastier the salad). Or opt for the ready-made coleslaw. Last minute "do's" while the chops broil include heating the carrots, finishing up the salad and stirring up instant mashed potatoes. Dessert is a refreshing just-before-serving fruit and sherbet fix-up.

SMOKED PORK CHOPS

Diagonally slash outer edge of fat on four ½-inch-thick smoked pork chops at 1-inch intervals to prevent curling. Set oven control at broil and/or 550°. Broil chops with tops 3 to 5 inches from heat until done, about 6 minutes on each side.

2 servings.

Note: To panfry, rub 8-inch skillet with fat cut from chops. Cook chops over medium heat until done, about 3 minutes on each side.

PARSLEY-BUTTERED CARROTS

1 can (16 ounces) whole small
   carrots
1 tablespoon butter or margarine
1 teaspoon parsley flakes

Heat carrots (with liquid); drain. Dot with butter. Sprinkle with parsley flakes and toss.

2 servings.

Note: Use the vegetable cooking liquid in soups, gravies and sauces whenever possible, as it contains vitamins and minerals.

SAUERKRAUT SALAD

1 can (8 ounces) sauerkraut, rinsed
   and well drained
¼ cup chopped green pepper
1 tablespoon chopped red onion
1 tablespoon sugar
¼ teaspoon caraway seed
¼ teaspoon salt
   Dash pepper
2 tablespoons oil-and-vinegar
   dressing
   Crisp salad greens

Toss all ingredients except salad greens in bowl. Cover and refrigerate at least 30 minutes. Drain. Serve on salad greens.

2 servings.

Time-savers: Substitute 1 tablespoon dried mixed salad onions for the red onion and 1 teaspoon dried green bell pepper for the fresh pepper.

APPLE SLAW

1 pint coleslaw (from delicatessen)
1 red apple, chopped
   Crumbled blue cheese

Mix coleslaw and apple in bowl; garnish with cheese.

2 servings.

FROSTY SHERBET SANDWICHES

1 can (8 ounces) sliced pineapple,
   drained
   Orange sherbet or vanilla
   ice cream
   Apricot preserves
   Diced roasted almonds

Place 1 pineapple slice on each dessert plate; top each with a scoop of sherbet. Cut 1 side of each remaining pineapple slice; twist and place on sherbet. Drizzle preserves on each serving; sprinkle with almonds.

2 servings.

Smoked Pork Chops
Mashed Potatoes
Parsley-buttered Carrots
Sauerkraut Salad or
Apple Slaw
Frosty Sherbet Sandwiches

Think easy: Let the broiler do most of your work. Start the potatoes first. The broiler tends to the chops, zucchini and tomatoes.

HERBED LAMB CHOPS

2 to 4 lamb rib, loin or shoulder
  chops, ¾ to 1 inch thick
¼ teaspoon oregano, rosemary or
  marjoram
  Salt and pepper

Set oven control at broil and/or 550°. Diagonally slash outer edge of fat on chops at 1-inch intervals to prevent curling. Sprinkle oregano on chops. Place chops on rack in broiler pan. Broil with tops about 3 inches from heat until brown, about 6 minutes on each side. Season with salt and pepper. (Season after browning—salt tends to draw moisture to surface and delays browning.) Garnish with mint jelly.

2 servings.

QUICK AU GRATIN POTATOES

Measure contents of 1 package (5.5 ounces) au gratin potatoes; divide in half (approximately 1 cup potato slices and 3 tablespoons sauce mix).* Place half the potato slices in 1-quart saucepan; sprinkle 3 tablespoons sauce mix on potato slices. Stir in half the amounts of butter, water and milk called for on package. Heat to boiling, stirring occasionally. Reduce heat; cover and simmer until potatoes are tender, about 20 minutes.

2 servings.

*To store remaining mix, close package securely; use within 2 weeks. Prepare Quick au Gratin Potatoes again and serve with ham, frankfurters, meat loaf, meatballs or hamburgers.

BROILED ZUCCHINI

Set oven control at broil and/or 550°. Remove stem and blossom ends from 2 medium zucchini. Cut each zucchini lengthwise in half.

Place cut sides down on rack in broiler pan. Broil about 3 inches from heat 6 minutes. Turn zucchini and brush each cut side with melted butter or margarine; season with salt and pepper. Broil until tender, about 6 minutes longer.

2 servings.

BROILED TOMATOES

Set oven control at broil and/or 550°. Remove stem end from 1 medium tomato; cut tomato in half. Dot each half with ½ teaspoon butter or margarine; sprinkle with garlic salt, lemon pepper, and if desired, basil leaves, oregano leaves or savory. Broil tomato halves cut sides up with tops about 3 inches from heat until golden brown, about 5 minutes.

2 servings.

PEARS AU CHOCOLAT

1 can (8 ounces) pear halves,
  drained
⅛ teaspoon peppermint extract
½ can (17.5-ounce size) chocolate
  pudding (1 cup)

Place 2 pear halves in each dessert dish. Stir peppermint extract into pudding; spoon on pears. Garnish with dollop of whipped topping and maraschino cherry or mint leaf.

2 servings.

**London Broil
Mushroom Rice
Crisp Green Salad
Fresh Fruit and Cheese**

LONDON BROIL

Score 1-pound flank steak; place in shallow glass dish. Pour ½ cup Italian dressing on steak. Cover and refrigerate at least 8 hours, turning meat occasionally.

Remove steak; reserve dressing. Set oven control at broil and/or 550°. Broil steak with top 3 to 4 inches from heat until medium rare, about 4 minutes on each side, brushing with reserved dressing several times. Cut meat across grain at a slanted angle into thin slices.

2 generous servings.

Note: Any leftover steak is delicious served cold on buttered split French rolls. Top with crisp sliced relishes (green pepper rings, thinly sliced onions, sliced radishes, thinly sliced dill pickles) and your favorite sandwich sauce (horseradish sauce, mayonnaise, barbecue sauce, mustard).

MUSHROOM RICE

Uncooked instant rice
(enough for 2 servings)
1 teaspoon butter or margarine
1 can (2 ounces) mushroom stems
and pieces, drained
¼ teaspoon parsley flakes

Cook rice as directed on package. Stir in butter, mushrooms and parsley flakes; heat through, stirring occasionally.

2 servings.

FRESH FRUIT AND CHEESE

Serve a variety of fresh fruit and dessert cheeses (Gourmandise, Port du Salut, Swiss, Bel Paese, Cheddar, Gruyère, Edam, Gouda) on tray with dessert plates and small knives. Cheeses should be at room temperature.

BROILED HAM AND SWEET POTATOES

1 fully cooked smoked ham slice,
  about ½ inch thick
1 can (8 ounces) sweet potatoes
  in syrup, drained
2 canned pineapple slices, well drained*
2 tablespoons orange marmalade

Set oven control at broil and/or 550°
Diagonally slash outer edge of fat on ham
slice at 1-inch intervals to prevent curling.
Place ham slice on rack in broiler pan.
Broil ham slice with top 3 inches from heat
until light brown, about 5 minutes.

Turn ham; place potatoes and pineapple
on rack. Brush marmalade on potatoes and
pineapple. Broil until potatoes and pineapple are hot and ham is light brown,
about 5 minutes.

2 servings.

*Extra pineapple slices? Top with cottage
cheese for a salad or use in Pineapple
Burgers (page 11).

BRUSSELS SPROUTS WITH CASHEWS

Cook 1 package (10 ounces) frozen Brussels sprouts as directed. Drain and return
to saucepan. Add 2 tablespoons cashews,
walnuts or sliced water chestnuts and
1 tablespoon butter or margarine; heat
through.

2 servings.

LETTUCE WEDGES WITH
TANGY CORN DRESSING

Mix 2 tablespoons oil-and-vinegar dressing and ¼ cup corn relish.* Spoon on
lettuce wedges.

2 servings.

*Extra corn relish? Serve later in the week
as a zesty accompaniment for roast pork,
veal, ham or chicken.

BANANA FONDUE FRITTERS

1 cup buttermilk baking mix
½ cup water
1 egg
¼ teaspoon almond extract
  Salad oil
2 bananas, cut into ½-inch slices
  Confectioners' sugar

Beat baking mix, water, egg and extract
with rotary beater until smooth.

Pour oil into metal fondue pot to depth
of 1 to 1½ inches. Heat on fondue stand
over burner or on range to 375° or until
1-inch bread cube browns in 1 minute.

With long-handled fork, each person dips
banana slice into batter, cooks it in hot
oil until puffed and golden brown, then
rolls fritter in confectioners' sugar.

2 generous servings.

Variations

Apple Fondue Fritters: Substitute 2 apples,
pared and cut into ½-inch slices, for the
bananas. Roll fritters in cinnamon-sugar
mixture instead of in confectioners' sugar.

Strawberry Fondue Fritters: Substitute
½ pint fresh strawberries for the bananas.

Pineapple Fondue Fritters: Substitute 1
can (13½ ounces) pineapple chunks,
drained, for the bananas.

**Broiled Ham
and Sweet Potatoes
Brussels Sprouts
with Cashews
Lettuce Wedges
with Tangy Corn Dressing
Banana Fondue Fritters**

Something Special...

Quick Desserts

Top lemon or other sherbet with crème de menthe, fruit-flavored liqueur, grenadine, fruit jam or honey.

Top brownie wedges with vanilla ice cream, chocolate sauce and confetti candies.

In blender, mix 1 pint vanilla ice cream with 2 tablespoons grenadine, crème de menthe or apricot brandy.

Sprinkle fresh or canned fruits with orange-flavored liqueur or drizzle with partially thawed frozen fruit juice concentrate.

Top fresh strawberries with champagne, white wine or ginger ale.

Cut 2 wedges from a cantaloupe or honeydew melon. Garnish with kabobs of strawberries and pineapple chunks on picks.

Mix 1 cup canned vanilla pudding with ¼ cup dairy sour cream. Alternate layers of this with canned cherry (or other) pie filling.

Fill split ladyfingers with canned chocolate pudding. Sprinkle with confectioners' sugar and drizzle with fudge sauce.

Alternate layers of cake cubes, sliced strawberries and canned vanilla pudding. Garnish with whipped topping and almonds.

Ready to serve in 15 minutes? Believe it! Here's the sequence: Start with the salad, then on to the steaks. While the steaks are browning, get going on the mashed potatoes (from a mix) and vegetables. Dessert? You can put it together after the meal—it's that quick.

There's more to this meal than the speed and ease of it: suspense. For the pear filling, simply scrounge among your on-hand goodies. The same applies to dessert. If your shelf proffers pudding, go the Spanish Sundaes route. Or ad lib your way with the Cake Parfaits fixings.

MINUTE STEAKS WITH BUTTER SAUCE

1 tablespoon salad oil
2 beef cubed steaks
  Garlic salt
2 tablespoons butter or margarine
1 teaspoon lemon juice
1 teaspoon Worcestershire sauce
½ teaspoon freeze-dried chives
¼ teaspoon dry mustard

Heat oil in 8-inch skillet; cook steaks over medium-high heat until brown, about 4 minutes on each side. Season with garlic salt. Remove steaks from skillet and keep warm.

Drain off fat. Melt butter in same skillet. Stir in remaining ingredients and heat. Place steaks on dinner plates; pour butter mixture on each.

2 servings.

CHILI MIXED VEGETABLES

Cook ½ package (10-ounce size) frozen mixed vegetables* as directed except— use only half the amounts of water and salt called for on package. Drain. Add 1 tablespoon butter or margarine and ¼ teaspoon chili powder and toss.

2 servings.

*Leftover frozen vegetables? Use in Shepherds' Pie (page 87). Or cook the entire package; season half as directed above and marinate the other half with salad dressing to serve as a salad the next day.

STUFFED PEAR SALAD

Drain 1 can (8 ounces) pear halves. Arrange on crisp salad greens. Fill centers of pear halves with cranberry sauce or relish, raspberry or strawberry jelly, fruit-flavored gelatin cubes or peanut butter.

2 servings.

CAKE PARFAITS

Cut pound cake (from freezer), leftover Quick Date Cake (page 62) or fig bars into cubes. Layer cubes alternately in parfait glasses with one of the following:

Apricot or pineapple yogurt.

Orange sherbet.

Vanilla ice cream and chocolate sauce.

Whipped topping and grated orange peel.

2 servings.

SPANISH SUNDAES

Divide ½ can (17.5-ounce size) vanilla pudding (1 cup) between dessert dishes. Drizzle chocolate syrup or sauce on each and top with Spanish peanuts.

2 servings.

Minute Steaks with Butter Sauce
Mashed Potatoes
Chili Mixed Vegetables
Stuffed Pear Salad
Cake Parfaits or Spanish Sundaes

Suppose you *are* held up in traffic coming home? With this dinner plan, you can make it to the table in less than half an hour. Use frozen green beans, of course—perhaps with a crunchy sprinkling of almonds. The cake dessert's out of the freezer, too. Another day, another hold-up, another meal: the chicken livers on toasted English muffin halves or hot rice and the exotic Nesselrode dessert.

CHICKEN LIVERS WITH MUSHROOMS

½ pound fresh or frozen chicken
   livers
2 tablespoons butter or margarine
1 can (2 ounces) mushroom stems
   and pieces
¼ cup water
1 tablespoon flour
¼ teaspoon salt
⅛ teaspoon pepper
1 teaspoon parsley flakes
1 teaspoon instant chicken bouillon
   or 1 chicken bouillon cube
   Toast points

If using frozen chicken livers, thaw as directed on package or quick-thaw (see note below). Cut livers into halves if necessary.

Melt butter in 8-inch skillet; brown livers over medium heat, stirring occasionally, 3 to 4 minutes. Stir in mushrooms (with liquid) and remaining ingredients except toast points. Heat to boiling. Reduce heat; simmer uncovered, stirring occasionally, until livers are done, about 5 minutes. Serve on toast points.

2 servings.

Note: To quick-thaw livers, place them in melted butter in skillet. Cover and cook over medium heat until livers are thawed and can be easily separated, about 15 minutes. Remove cover; cook until livers are brown.

TOMATO-GRAPEFRUIT SALAD

1 can (8 ounces) grapefruit sections,
   drained
1 tomato, cut into wedges
   Salad greens
   Green pepper strips
   Clear sweet-and-sour dressing

Arrange grapefruit sections and tomato wedges on salad greens. Top salads with green pepper strips and drizzle with dressing.

2 servings.

Variation

Tomato-Pineapple Salad: Substitute 2 pine-apple slices for the grapefruit sections and cut tomato into slices.

BUTTERSCOTCH CAKE SUNDAES

2 slices pound cake (from
   freezer) or leftover Gingerbread
   (page 35) or 2 commercially
   prepared sponge shortcakes
   Vanilla ice cream
   Butterscotch ice-cream topping

Place cake slices on dessert plates; top with scoops of ice cream. Drizzle ice-cream topping on each.

2 servings.

NESSELRODE SUNDAES

Heat ¼ cup Nesselrode mixture,* stirring occasionally. Soak 2 sugar cubes in orange extract 2 to 3 minutes. Place scoop of vanilla ice cream in each dessert dish. Spoon hot Nesselrode mixture on ice cream. Place a sugar cube on top of each sundae and ignite.

2 servings.

*Extra Nesselrode? Use as a topping for vanilla, rice or tapioca pudding, lemon sherbet, pound cake or gingerbread. Or make Nesselrode Ice Cream (page 70).

To ready this dinner in half an hour, start it in the middle. Do your chop-chop with the cabbage first to give it time to drain. Then let the oven do double duty, "frying" the fish and heating the potatoes. Dessert? If custard's your choice, chill the pudding when you chop the cabbage; for the compote, a quick late-heating is all you need.

OVEN-FRIED PIKE

1 pound fresh or frozen pike fillets
2 tablespoons butter or margarine
½ teaspoon salt
¼ teaspoon pepper
¼ cup all-purpose flour or
    buttermilk baking mix
    Paprika
    Tomato wedges
    Lemon wedges

Heat oven to 500°. If using frozen fillets, thaw as directed on package. In oven, melt butter in shallow baking dish. Sprinkle salt and pepper on fish, then coat with flour and place in baking dish. Sprinkle paprika on fish. Bake uncovered until fish flakes easily with fork, 10 to 15 minutes. Garnish with tomato and lemon wedges.

2 servings.

LEMON-CHIVE POTATOES

1 can (about 16 ounces) whole
    potatoes
1 tablespoon butter or margarine
2 teaspoons lemon juice
½ teaspoon freeze-dried chives

Heat oven to 500°. Drain and rinse potatoes; place in ungreased 1-quart casserole. Cover potatoes with water. Cover and bake until potatoes are hot, 10 to 15 minutes. Drain. Add remaining ingredients and toss until potatoes are coated.

2 servings.

CABBAGE-GREEN PEPPER SLAW

⅛ medium green cabbage, cut into
    pieces
½ small green pepper, cut into
    pieces
2 green onions, cut into pieces
½ teaspoon salt
2 tablespoons coleslaw dressing

Place cabbage, green pepper and onions in blender; cover with cold water. Chop 3 to 5 seconds. Drain thoroughly in colander or sieve. Mix vegetables, salt and dressing.

2 servings.

PEACHES 'N CUSTARD

½ cup canned vanilla pudding
2 teaspoons orange juice
1 can (8 ounces) sliced peaches,
    drained
1 teaspoon currant jelly

Mix pudding and orange juice; chill. Divide peach slices between dessert dishes. Spoon pudding mixture onto peaches and top each serving with ½ teaspoon jelly.

2 servings.

SPICED FRUIT COMPOTE

1 can (8 ounces) fruit cocktail or
    fruits for salad
⅛ teaspoon allspice

Heat fruit cocktail (with syrup) and allspice to boiling. Serve warm.

2 servings.

Oven-fried Pike
Lemon-Chive Potatoes
Buttered Green Beans
Cabbage-Green Pepper Slaw
Peaches 'n Custard or Spiced Fruit Compote

A super supper for a superhot night—or any time you're in the mood for cool elegance. The Cheese-Onion Twists can be baked ahead (even frozen ahead). Just wrap in foil and pop into a 350° oven for 10 minutes, 20 to 25 minutes if frozen.

HOT TOMATO BOUILLON

¾ cup tomato juice
¼ cup water
1 beef bouillon cube

Heat all ingredients over medium-high heat to boiling, stirring occasionally. Serve hot.

2 servings.

SEAFOOD SALAD BOWL

1 can (4½ ounces) large shrimp, rinsed and drained
1 can (7½ ounces) crabmeat, drained and cartilage removed
6 cups bite-size pieces lettuce (iceberg, Bibb, romaine, leaf)
½ jar (6-ounce size) marinated artichoke hearts, drained
¼ cup sliced pitted ripe olives
1 hard-cooked egg, cut into wedges
½ teaspoon capers, if desired
Freshly ground black pepper
Italian dressing or creamy French dressing

Reserve some shrimp and crabmeat pieces for garnish. Toss remaining shrimp, crabmeat, the lettuce, artichoke hearts and olives. Divide between salad bowls. Garnish with reserved shrimp and crabmeat pieces, the egg wedges, capers and pepper. Serve with dressing.

2 generous servings.

Note: You can substitute 1 can (about 5 ounces) lobster or 1 can (6½ ounces) tuna for the shrimp or crabmeat.

CHEESE-ONION TWISTS

2 teaspoons instant minced onion
1 tablespoon butter or margarine, softened
2 tablespoons shredded Cheddar cheese
½ cup buttermilk baking mix
2 tablespoons water
Soft butter or margarine
Caraway seed, dill weed or poppy seed

Heat oven to 425°. Mix onion, 1 tablespoon butter and the cheese. Stir baking mix and water with fork to soft dough. Turn onto lightly floured cloth-covered board; smooth dough into ball and knead about 5 times. Pat or roll into rectangle, 8x6 inches.

Spread onion mixture on rectangle to within 2 inches of one long side. Beginning with plain side, fold lengthwise into thirds; press together. Cut crosswise into 6 strips. Twist each strip twice.

Place twists on ungreased baking sheet; press ends on sheet to fasten securely. Brush soft butter on twists; sprinkle with caraway seed. Bake until light brown, about 10 minutes. Serve warm.

6 twists.

ORANGE SLUSH

In blender or small mixer bowl, mix 1 pint vanilla ice cream, softened, and ¼ cup frozen orange juice concentrate (thawed) until thick and smooth. Garnish each drink with orange slice and mint leaves. Serve with straws.

2 servings.

Dinner in a jiffy—and not a skimp in sight. With a little bit of planning, this lamb patty broiler menu can make it from start to serve in 20 minutes, maybe less. Begin with the patties, turn, then snuggle the eggplant slices around them. All will finish hot and tender and together. Then while dinner plates are being cleared, run the dessert sauce under the broiler for a hot, bubbly finale. Quick-and-easy cooking—quick-and-easy cleaning.

Broiled Lamb Patties
Broiled Eggplant with Tomato Sauce
Wilted French Onion Salad
Warm Apricot Crunch Sundaes

BROILED LAMB PATTIES

2 lamb patties (4 ounces each)
  Salt
  Lemon pepper

Set oven control at broil and/or 550°. Place patties on rack in broiler pan. Broil with tops 3 to 5 inches from heat until brown, about 7 minutes. Sprinkle with salt and lemon pepper. Turn patties; broil until medium done, about 7 minutes.

2 servings.

BROILED EGGPLANT WITH TOMATO SAUCE

1 small eggplant (about 1 pound), pared and cut into ½-inch slices
  Soft butter or margarine
  Salt and pepper
1 can (8 ounces) tomato sauce
¼ teaspoon garlic powder

Set oven control at broil and/or 550°. Place eggplant slices on rack in broiler pan. Brush butter on slices; season with salt and pepper. Broil with tops about 3 inches from heat until eggplant is hot and tender, about 6 minutes.

In small saucepan, heat tomato sauce and garlic powder, stirring occasionally. Serve on eggplant slices.

2 servings.

WILTED FRENCH ONION SALAD

1 small onion, thinly sliced and separated into rings
2 to 4 cups bite-size pieces romaine
¼ cup oil-and-vinegar dressing
2 teaspoons sugar
½ teaspoon instant beef bouillon
  Dash red pepper sauce
  Grated Parmesan or Swiss cheese
  Seasoned croutons

Toss onion rings and romaine in salad bowls. In small saucepan, heat dressing, sugar, bouillon and red pepper sauce to boiling, stirring occasionally. Drizzle hot dressing on salads; sprinkle with cheese and croutons.

2 servings.

WARM APRICOT CRUNCH SUNDAES

1 can (8 ounces) apricot halves, drained
2 tablespoons brown sugar
¼ cup cashew halves
1 tablespoon soft butter or margarine
  Vanilla ice cream

Set oven control at broil and/or 550°. Place apricots in 8-inch ovenproof skillet or shallow baking dish. Sprinkle sugar and cashews on apricots; dot with butter. Broil with tops about 6 inches from heat until sugar and butter are melted and sauce is bubbly, about 2 minutes. Serve immediately on ice cream.

2 servings.

more dimes than dollars

Inventive dinners that make
the most of a little money

Economy and elegance make an enticing combination, you must admit. (Take a look at the photograph on page 25.) After browning, you can transfer these chops to a 9x9x2-inch baking pan (ungreased), cover with foil and bake at 350° for 45 minutes.

Pork Chops Creole
Buttered Green Beans
Peanut Crunch Slaw
Cloverleaf Rolls
Mocha Parfaits

PORK CHOPS CREOLE

4 pork loin or rib chops, ½ to ¾
   inch thick
1 teaspoon salt
¼ teaspoon pepper
4 thin onion slices
4 green pepper rings
4 tablespoons uncooked instant rice
1 can (8 ounces) stewed tomatoes

In 10-inch skillet, brown chops over medium heat. Sprinkle salt and pepper on chops. Top each with 1 onion slice, 1 green pepper ring, 1 tablespoon rice and ¼ cup tomatoes. Reduce heat; cover and simmer until done, about 45 minutes. (Add small amount of water if necessary.)

2 servings.

PEANUT CRUNCH SLAW

2 tablespoons mayonnaise
2 tablespoons dairy sour cream
½ teaspoon salt
2 tablespoons chopped green onion
2 tablespoons chopped green pepper
¼ cup chopped cucumber
1 cup shredded cabbage
¼ cup thinly sliced celery
2 tablespoons chopped salted peanuts
   Grated Parmesan cheese

Mix mayonnaise, sour cream, salt, onion, green pepper and cucumber in bowl. Stir in cabbage and celery. Sprinkle peanuts and cheese on each serving.

2 servings.

MOCHA PARFAITS

¼ cup chilled whipping cream or
   ½ cup frozen whipped topping
   (thawed)
2 teaspoons sugar
½ teaspoon powdered instant coffee
½ can (17.5-ounce size) chocolate
   pudding (1 cup)

In chilled bowl, beat whipping cream, sugar and instant coffee until stiff. (If using whipped topping, omit sugar and mix in instant coffee.) Alternate layers of pudding and whipped cream in parfait glasses or dessert dishes. Chill. Garnish with chocolate shot or chocolate curls.

2 servings.

Something to Know About...

To make chocolate curls, place a large milk chocolate bar on a flat surface. Draw a vegetable parer along the bar toward you, making long, thin strokes. The job will be easier if the chocolate bar is slightly soft. Use a wooden pick to lift the curls so they won't break, as they're fragile.

Here's a duo you may not have thought of before. Saucily seasoned fish and Parmesan-topped potatoes make memorable broiler-mates. Try! P.S. The dedicated dimes versus dollars cook will cut up the fudgy cake for luscious freeze-aheads. Like money in the bank.

BROILED FISH AND TATERS

1 pound fresh or frozen cod, perch or flounder fillets
2 tablespoons butter or margarine, melted
1 tablespoon lemon juice
2 tablespoons catsup
½ teaspoon Worcestershire sauce
½ teaspoon salt
⅛ teaspoon dry mustard
2 cooked pared medium potatoes, cut into ⅜-inch slices
2 tablespoons butter or margarine, melted
3 tablespoons grated Parmesan cheese

Thaw fillets if frozen; cut into serving pieces. Set oven control at broil and/or 550°. Place fish on greased rack in broiler pan. Mix 2 tablespoons butter, the lemon juice, catsup, Worcestershire sauce, salt and mustard; brush part of sauce on fish. Broil fish with tops 4 inches from heat 8 minutes, brushing with sauce once or twice.

Turn fish; brush with remaining sauce. Arrange potato slices on broiler rack. Brush 2 tablespoons butter on potatoes and sprinkle with cheese. Broil until fish flakes easily with fork and potatoes are golden brown, about 5 minutes.

2 servings.

Time-saver: No cooked potatoes on hand —and no time to cook them? Use ½ package (14-ounce size) frozen sliced panfried or French fried potatoes instead.

BROWN BEAUTY CAKE

1 cup all-purpose flour* or cake flour
1 cup sugar
½ teaspoon soda
½ teaspoon salt
¼ teaspoon baking powder
¼ cup water
½ cup buttermilk
¼ cup shortening
1 egg
½ teaspoon vanilla
2 ounces melted unsweetened chocolate (cool)
Fudge Frosting (below)

Heat oven to 350°. Grease and flour baking pan, 8x8x2 or 9x9x2 inches. Into large mixer bowl, measure all ingredients except Fudge Frosting. Blend on low speed ½ minute, scraping bowl constantly. Beat on high speed 3 minutes, scraping bowl occasionally. Pour into pan.

Bake until wooden pick inserted in center comes out clean, 30 to 35 minutes. Cool. Frost with Fudge Frosting.

*If using self-rising flour, omit soda, salt and baking powder.

Fudge Frosting

¼ cup shortening
1 cup sugar
2 squares (1 ounce each) unsweetened chocolate
⅓ cup milk
¼ teaspoon salt
1 teaspoon vanilla

In 2-quart saucepan, heat all ingredients except vanilla to rolling boil, stirring occasionally. Boil 1 minute without stirring. Place pan in bowl of ice and water; beat frosting until cool and of spreading consistency. Stir in vanilla.

Enough frosting for 8- or 9-inch square cake.

Broiled Fish and Taters
Buttered Peas
Cabbage Slaw (page 41)
Brown Beauty Cake with Fudge Frosting

EGGS DELMONICO

1 can (10½ ounces) condensed cream of mushroom or cream of chicken soup
½ cup shredded natural Cheddar cheese
3 or 4 hard-cooked eggs, sliced
1 tablespoon finely chopped pimiento
  Hot buttered toast or toasted English muffins
  Paprika or snipped parsley

In 1-quart saucepan, heat soup over medium heat until hot and bubbly, 3 to 5 minutes. Stir in cheese; cook over low heat, stirring occasionally, until cheese is melted. Fold in eggs and pimiento; heat through, about 2 minutes. Serve on toast; sprinkle paprika on top.

2 servings.

Variation
Creamed Eggs with Tuna: Use only 2 eggs and fold in 1 can (3¼ ounces) tuna, drained and flaked.

NUTMEG SPINACH

1 pound fresh spinach
½ teaspoon salt
⅛ teaspoon nutmeg
  Dash lemon pepper
1 tablespoon butter or margarine

Remove imperfect leaves and root ends of spinach. Wash spinach; drain and place in large saucepan with just the water which clings to leaves. Cover and cook until spinach is wilted, 3 to 5 minutes. Drain. Stir in salt, nutmeg, lemon pepper and butter.

2 servings.

Time-saver: Cook 1 package (10 ounces) frozen chopped spinach as directed; drain and season with nutmeg, lemon pepper and butter.

APPLE-ORANGE PINWHEEL SALAD

1 red apple
1 orange, pared and sectioned
  Crisp salad greens
  Honey Dressing (below)

Cut unpared apple into wedges. Arrange apple wedges and orange sections in pinwheel design on salad greens. Drizzle Honey Dressing on fruit.

2 servings.

Honey Dressing
Mix ¼ cup mayonnaise or salad dressing, 2 tablespoons honey and 1½ teaspoons lemon juice.

COFFEE CRUNCH BARS

1 cup all-purpose flour*
½ cup brown sugar (packed)
½ cup butter or margarine, softened
2 to 3 teaspoons powdered instant coffee
¼ teaspoon baking powder
⅛ teaspoon salt
½ teaspoon vanilla
¼ cup chopped walnuts
½ cup semisweet chocolate pieces

Heat oven to 350°. Mix flour, sugar, butter, coffee, baking powder, salt and vanilla. Stir in nuts and chocolate pieces. Press mixture evenly into ungreased baking pan, 9x9x2 inches. Bake until light brown and crisp, 20 to 25 minutes. Cut into bars, 3x1½ inches, while warm.

18 bars.

*If using self-rising flour, omit baking powder and salt.

Eggs Delmonico
Nutmeg Spinach
Apple-Orange Pinwheel Salad
Coffee Crunch Bars

Honestly, now, would you peg this meal as a penny-squeezer? Double it when you have another twosome over and see if they don't say, "Magnifico!" One reason: You cared enough to make those butter sticks from "scratch." And there's that special salad, too. As for dessert, it's one of the more costly ones when you order it in an Italian restaurant. Yet it takes so little time (and money) to make it at home this easy way.

ITALIAN SPAGHETTI

½ pound ground beef
3 tablespoons minced onion
1 can (8 ounces) tomato sauce
1 can (6 ounces) tomato paste
1 cup water
¼ teaspoon salt
¼ teaspoon garlic powder
¼ teaspoon oregano leaves
¼ teaspoon basil
3½ to 4 ounces uncooked spaghetti
    Grated Parmesan cheese

In 8-inch skillet, cook and stir meat until brown. Stir in remaining ingredients except spaghetti and cheese. Heat to boiling. Reduce heat; cover and simmer 1 hour. While sauce simmers, cook spaghetti as directed on package. Serve sauce on hot spaghetti; pass Parmesan cheese.

2 servings.

TOSSED SPINACH SALAD

2 cups bite-size pieces spinach
    leaves (about 5 ounces)
2 or 3 radishes, sliced
2 slices onion, separated into rings
    Oil-and-vinegar dressing

Toss spinach, radish slices and onion rings in bowl. Serve salad with oil-and-vinegar dressing.

2 servings.

BUTTER STICKS

¼ cup butter or margarine
1 cup buttermilk baking mix
¼ cup water
    Salt

Heat oven to 425°. In oven, melt butter in baking pan, 9x9x2 inches. Stir baking mix and water with fork to a soft dough. Turn onto floured cloth-covered board; smooth dough into ball and knead 5 times. Roll into rectangle, 6x4 inches. Cut into 8 strips, 4x¾ inch.

Dip each strip into melted butter, coating all sides, and arrange in pan. Sprinkle salt lightly on strips. Bake until golden brown, 10 to 12 minutes.

8 sticks.

BISCUIT TORTONI

2 tablespoons vanilla wafer or
    macaroon crumbs
1 tablespoon diced candied or
    well-drained maraschino cherries
2 tablespoons diced roasted
    almonds
½ pint vanilla ice cream (1 cup)

Line 2 muffin cups with paper baking cups. Mix crumbs, cherries and almonds. Soften ice cream slightly; fold in crumb mixture. Divide ice-cream mixture between muffin cups. Decorate each with red cherry half and slices of green cherry to resemble a flower. Freeze until firm.

2 servings.

Italian Spaghetti
Tossed Spinach Salad
Butter Sticks
Biscuit Tortoni

Viva round steak! When a mere ½ pound of same can inspire such a savory, satisfying dish, the economy bit almost becomes a joy. The salad's a refreshing contrast to the spicy main dish, and the sundaes are gloriously rich. (If you can't buy cinnamon ice cream, see our quick fix-up on page 70.)

MEXICAN STEAK 'N BEANS

½ pound beef round steak,
   ½ to ¾ inch thick
1 tablespoon flour
½ to 1 teaspoon chili powder
¼ teaspoon salt
⅛ teaspoon pepper
⅛ teaspoon ground cumin, if
   desired
1 tablespoon salad oil
½ cup water
¼ cup chili sauce
¾ cup sliced celery
1 medium onion, chopped (about
   ½ cup)
1 carrot, cut diagonally into ½-inch
   slices
1 small green pepper, cut into
   ¼-inch strips
1 can (8 ounces) kidney beans

Cut meat into 1-inch pieces. Mix flour, chili powder, salt, pepper and cumin; coat meat with flour mixture.

Heat oil in 8-inch skillet; brown meat over medium heat, about 10 minutes. Drain off fat. Stir in water, chili sauce, celery and onion; heat to boiling. Reduce heat; cover and simmer until meat is almost tender, 30 to 45 minutes. (Add small amount of water if necessary.)

Add carrot; cover and simmer 20 minutes. Stir in green pepper and beans (with liquid); cover and simmer until green pepper is crisp-tender and beans are hot, about 10 minutes.

2 servings.

ORANGE-CUCUMBER SALAD

1 orange, pared and sectioned
1 medium cucumber, sliced
1 small onion, sliced and
   separated into rings
   Orange Dressing (page 68)
   or French dressing
   Crisp salad greens

Toss orange sections, cucumber slices, onion rings and Orange Dressing in bowl. Cover and refrigerate 1 to 2 hours. To serve, remove salad with slotted spoon to salad greens.

2 servings.

HOT FUDGE-CINNAMON SUNDAES

Prepare Hot Fudge Sauce (below) or heat about ¼ cup commercially prepared chocolate sauce. Spoon ¼ cup hot sauce on scoops of cinnamon or vanilla ice cream.

2 servings.

Hot Fudge Sauce

¾ cup light cream (20%) or
   evaporated milk
1 cup sugar
2 ounces unsweetened chocolate
2 tablespoons butter or margarine
½ teaspoon vanilla
¼ teaspoon salt

Heat cream and sugar to rolling boil, stirring constantly. Boil and stir 1 minute. Reduce heat; add chocolate and stir until chocolate is melted and sauce is smooth. (If sauce has slightly curdled appearance, beat until creamy smooth.) Remove from heat; stir in butter, vanilla and salt.

1½ cups.

Note: Refrigerate leftover sauce in covered container. To use again, reheat over low heat, stirring constantly.

CRUSTY CURRIED CHICKEN WITH BISCUITS

2 tablespoons salad oil
½ cup buttermilk baking mix
1 tablespoon curry powder
1 teaspoon salt
⅛ teaspoon pepper
1½ pounds chicken pieces or 2-pound broiler-fryer chicken, quartered
1 cup buttermilk baking mix
¼ cup water
2 canned peach halves, if desired

Heat oven to 425°. Pour oil into baking pan, 9x9x2 or 11¾x7½x1½ inches. Mix ½ cup baking mix, the curry powder, salt and pepper; coat chicken with mixture. Place chicken skin side down in pan. Bake uncovered 35 minutes.

Mix 1 cup baking mix and the water to a soft dough. Turn chicken, pushing pieces to one side of pan. Drop dough by spoonfuls (5) into pan in single layer next to chicken. Arrange peaches on chicken. Bake until biscuits are light brown and chicken is tender, about 15 minutes.

2 servings.

Variations

Gaucho Chicken with Chived Biscuits: Substitute 2 teaspoons chili powder for the curry powder; before mixing biscuit dough, add 1½ teaspoons snipped chives to baking mix.

Herbed Chicken with Biscuits: Substitute ¼ teaspoon thyme leaves and ¼ teaspoon rosemary leaves for the curry powder.

Crusty Curried Chicken with Biscuits
Buttered Broccoli
Green Bean-Tomato Vinaigrette
Frosted Melon Wedges with Berries

BUTTERED BROCCOLI

Trim off large leaves of ¾ to 1 pound broccoli; remove tough ends of lower stems. Wash broccoli. If stems are thicker than 1 inch in diameter, make lengthwise gashes in each stem.

Heat 1 inch salted water (½ teaspoon salt to 1 cup water) to boiling. Add broccoli; cover and heat to boiling. Cook until stems are tender, 12 to 15 minutes. Drain; dot with 1 tablespoon butter or margarine.

2 servings.

GREEN BEAN-TOMATO VINAIGRETTE

1 can (8 ounces) cut green beans, drained
¼ pint cherry tomatoes, cut into halves
1 small onion, sliced
1 can (2 ounces) sliced mushrooms, drained
¼ cup Italian dressing

Toss all ingredients together in bowl. Cover and chill at least 2 hours, tossing occasionally.

2 servings.

FROSTED MELON WEDGES WITH BERRIES

Place scoop of your favorite sherbet in center of each of 2 melon wedges; top each with ¼ cup berries. Here are some combinations you might like:

Honeydew melon, lemon or pineapple sherbet, raspberries or strawberries.

Cantaloupe or Persian melon, orange sherbet, blackberries.

Crenshaw melon, lime sherbet, blueberries or blackberries.

2 servings.

POT ROAST WITH CARROTS AND ONIONS

2 tablespoons salad oil
2-pound beef chuck pot roast
½ teaspoon salt
¼ teaspoon pepper
½ cup water
4 medium carrots, halved
   lengthwise
4 small onions
¼ teaspoon salt
   Kettle Gravy (below), if desired

Heat oil in Dutch oven or large skillet; brown meat over medium heat, about 15 minutes. Sprinkle ½ teaspoon salt and the pepper on meat. Add water; cover tightly and simmer on range or in 325° oven 1½ hours. (Add small amount of water if necessary.) Add vegetables and ¼ teaspoon salt; cook until meat is tender and vegetables are done, about ½ hour.

Place meat and vegetables on warm platter; keep warm while making gravy. Serve meat with gravy.

2 servings.

Kettle Gravy

Skim excess fat from meat broth. Measure broth; if necessary add enough water (or vegetable cooking liquid, consommé or vegetable juice) to measure ½ cup and pour into pan. Mix 2 tablespoons cold water and 1 tablespoon flour. Stir flour mixture into broth. Heat to boiling, stirring constantly. Boil and stir 1 minute. If desired, stir in few drops bottled brown bouquet sauce. Season with salt and pepper. If you prefer a thinner gravy, stir in small amount of additional liquid.

½ cup.

Note: If using quick-mixing flour, just stir into cold water with fork. If using regular flour, shake water and flour in covered jar—be sure to put water in jar first, then the flour.

HERBED NOODLES

3 to 4 ounces uncooked noodles
   (1 to 1½ cups)
¼ teaspoon thyme leaves
¼ teaspoon basil leaves
¼ teaspoon snipped parsley
¼ teaspoon snipped chives or
   finely chopped onion
1 tablespoon butter or
   margarine, melted

Cook noodles in 1 quart boiling salted water (1½ teaspoons salt) until tender, 7 to 10 minutes. Drain noodles and return to saucepan. Mix remaining ingredients; pour onto noodles and toss.

2 servings.

WARM CARAMEL PEARS

1 can (8 ounces) pear halves
   Vanilla ice cream
¼ teaspoon cinnamon
¼ cup caramel ice-cream topping

Heat pears (with syrup) in small saucepan. Drain. Spoon pears into serving dishes. Top with scoops of ice cream. Stir cinnamon into caramel topping; pour on each serving.

2 servings.

**Pot Roast
with Carrots and Onions
Herbed Noodles
Tossed Green Salad
Whole Wheat Rolls
Warm Caramel Pears**

Something to Know About...

To insure that Kettle Gravy will be smooth, stir constantly as you add the flour-water to the broth. The broth will have more flavor and color if the meat was browned slowly.

Barleyburger Stew
Hot French Bread
Fresh Vegetable Relishes
(page 46)
Velvet Crumb Cake with
Pineapple Sauce

BARLEYBURGER STEW

½ pound ground beef
½ cup chopped onion
¼ cup chopped celery
1 can (18 ounces) tomato juice
  (2¼ cups)
½ cup water
1 teaspoon salt
1 to 1½ teaspoons chili powder
¼ teaspoon pepper
¼ cup uncooked barley

In 3-quart saucepan, cook and stir meat and onion until meat is brown and onion is tender. Drain off fat. Stir in remaining ingredients; heat to boiling. Reduce heat; cover and simmer until barley is done and stew is desired consistency, about 1 hour.

2 servings.

VELVET CRUMB CAKE WITH PINEAPPLE SAUCE

⅓ cup brown sugar (packed)
2 teaspoons cornstarch
1 can (8½ ounces) crushed
  pineapple
2 servings Velvet Crumb Cake
  (page 73) or pound cake or 2
  commercially prepared sponge
  shortcakes

Mix sugar and cornstarch in small saucepan. Stir in pineapple (with syrup). Cook over medium heat, stirring constantly, until mixture thickens and boils. Boil and stir 1 minute. Serve warm sauce on cake. Top with whipped topping or whipped cream if you like.

2 servings.

SKILLET MACARONI AND CHEESE

3 tablespoons butter or margarine
½ package (7.25-ounce size)
  macaroni and cheese*
2 tablespoons chopped green
  pepper
1½ cups hot water
½ to ¾ cup cubed cooked ham or
  pork luncheon meat
½ teaspoon dry mustard
2 tablespoons chopped pimiento,
  if desired

Melt butter in 8-inch skillet. Cook and stir macaroni and green pepper over medium heat until macaroni is light golden, 3 to 5 minutes. Stir in water. Cover and simmer until macaroni is tender, about 15 minutes. Stir in meat, Sauce Mix and mustard. Simmer, stirring constantly, until meat is hot and cheese sauce is thickened, about 2 minutes. Stir in pimiento.

2 servings.

*To use half the package, measure contents and divide in half (approximately ¾ cup macaroni and 2 tablespoons Sauce Mix). To store remaining mix, close package securely and use within 2 weeks.

SCALLOPED TOMATOES

1 can (8 ounces) stewed
  tomatoes
⅛ teaspoon salt
⅛ teaspoon sugar
  Dash pepper
1 teaspoon butter or
  margarine
⅓ cup seasoned croutons

In small saucepan, heat tomatoes, salt, sugar and pepper to boiling. Reduce heat; cover and simmer 5 minutes. Stir in butter; sprinkle croutons on top.

2 servings.

GINGERBREAD STACKS
WITH HOT BUTTERSCOTCH SAUCE

½ package (14.5-ounce size)
  gingerbread mix*
½ cup lukewarm water
¼ cup butterscotch ice-cream
  topping
  Vanilla ice cream

Heat oven to 350°. Grease and flour loaf pan, 9x5x3 inches. In small mixer bowl, mix gingerbread mix and lukewarm water on low speed. Beat on medium speed 2 minutes, scraping bowl frequently, or beat 300 strokes by hand. Pour into pan. Bake until wooden pick inserted in center comes out clean, 15 to 20 minutes.

Heat butterscotch topping. Cut 2 servings from gingerbread; split each piece. (Use remaining gingerbread as suggested below.) Fill layers with ice cream; top with hot butterscotch topping.

2 servings.

*To use half the package, measure contents and divide in half (approximately 1½ cups). To store remaining mix, close package securely and use within 3 weeks to make hot gingerbread. Or make the entire package at one time and freeze leftover gingerbread for use as needed. Top it with applesauce and dash of cinnamon, whipped topping and sliced bananas, lemon sauce and cream cheese, vanilla ice cream and chocolate sauce or peach slices and mocha whipped cream.

Skillet Macaroni and Cheese
Scalloped Tomatoes
Marinated Green Bean Salad (page 55)
Hard Rolls
Gingerbread Stacks with Hot Butterscotch Sauce

When your dimes have to roll up their sleeves, hamburger can be a valiant helper. Especially in a quick-to-the-oven dish like this. Of course, you've made dessert ahead, so you simply sit back and relax. (Who could blame you for looking a touch smug?)

Deep-dish Hamburger Pie
Cabbage Slaw (page 41)
Garlic Bun Sticks
Cherry-Berry Parfaits

DEEP-DISH HAMBURGER PIE

½ pound ground beef
¼ cup chopped onion
¼ teaspoon salt
⅛ teaspoon pepper
¼ teaspoon monosodium glutamate
1 can (8 ounces) cut green beans, drained
½ can (10¾-ounce size) condensed tomato soup or ½ cup catsup
1 cup mashed potatoes
3 tablespoons shredded natural Cheddar cheese

Heat oven to 350°. In 8-inch skillet, cook and stir meat and onion until meat is brown and onion is tender. Stir in seasonings, beans and soup. Pour into ungreased 1-quart casserole. Spoon mashed potatoes on mixture and top with cheese. Bake until mixture is hot and top is slightly brown, about 30 minutes.

2 servings.

Note: Leftover mashed potatoes can be used in this recipe. Or prepare instant mashed potatoes as directed on package for 2 servings.

GARLIC BUN STICKS

Heat oven to 350°. Brush soft butter or margarine on 1 split frankfurter bun or 2 slices bread. Sprinkle with garlic salt and cut into strips. Place on ungreased baking sheet. Bake until golden brown, about 15 minutes.

2 servings.

CHERRY-BERRY PARFAITS

1 cup boiling water
1 package (3 ounces) cherry- or strawberry-flavored gelatin
1 package (10 ounces) frozen strawberries
¼ cup cold water

Pour boiling water on gelatin in bowl; stir until gelatin is dissolved. Stir in frozen strawberries until thawed. Stir in cold water. Chill until thickened but not set, about 1½ hours.

Pour 1½ cups of the gelatin mixture into bowl; beat until light and fluffy. (Use remaining gelatin mixture as suggested below.) Divide between parfait glasses or dessert dishes. Chill until set, about 1 hour. Garnish with a dollop of whipped topping.

2 servings.

Note: You can use the remaining gelatin mixture for tomorrow's salad. Divide between 2 individual molds and chill until set. Or serve as a dessert if you like: Pour remaining gelatin mixture into small shallow container and chill until set. Cut gelatin into cubes and layer in parfait glasses with vanilla pudding or frozen whipped topping (thawed).

COUNTRY-FRIED CHICKEN

Salad oil
¼ cup all-purpose flour
½ teaspoon salt
⅛ teaspoon pepper
⅛ teaspoon paprika
1½ pounds chicken pieces or
2-pound broiler-fryer chicken,
quartered or cut up

Heat ¼ inch salad oil in large skillet. Mix flour, salt, pepper and paprika; coat chicken with flour mixture. Cook chicken in oil over medium heat until light brown, 15 to 20 minutes. Reduce heat; cover tightly and simmer until thickest pieces are tender, 20 to 25 minutes, turning chicken once or twice to assure even cooking. (Add small amount of water if necessary.) Remove cover the last 5 minutes of cooking time to crisp chicken.

2 servings.

PAN GRAVY

1 tablespoon drippings (fat
and juices)
1 tablespoon flour
½ to ¾ cup liquid (broth, milk,
vegetable liquid, water)
Salt and pepper

Remove meat to warm platter; keep warm while preparing gravy. Pour drippings into bowl, leaving brown particles in pan. Return 1 tablespoon drippings to pan. Mix in flour. Cook over low heat, stirring until mixture is smooth and bubbly. Remove from heat. Stir in liquid. Heat to boiling, stirring constantly. Boil and stir 1 minute. If desired, stir in few drops bottled brown bouquet sauce for color. Season with salt and pepper.

½ to ¾ cup.

LEMON-FRESH MUSHROOM SALAD

¼ pound fresh mushrooms, sliced
Lemon-Herb Marinade (below)
2 lettuce wedges
2 large tomato slices

Place mushrooms in glass dish. Pour Lemon-Herb Marinade on mushrooms; cover and refrigerate up to 12 hours. Place lettuce wedge with tomato slice on each salad plate and top with mushrooms and small amount of marinade.

2 servings.

Lemon-Herb Marinade

¼ cup salad oil
¼ cup lemon juice
1 teaspoon seasoned salt
¼ teaspoon marjoram, basil or
oregano
⅛ teaspoon sugar
⅛ teaspoon garlic salt
Dash freshly ground pepper

Shake all ingredients together in tightly covered jar.

½ cup.

Country-fried Chicken
Pan Gravy
Mashed Potatoes
Green Peas
Lemon-Fresh Mushroom
Salad
Peach-Praline Shortcake
(page 53)

Something to Know About...

When you stir flour into pan drippings to make Pan Gravy, make sure you scrape in all the brown particles formed by cooking the meat—they're full of flavor and will give the gravy a deep-brown color. Don't forget that Pan Gravy can be made with the drippings of any meat that's been panfried, oven roasted or broiled, from pork chops to the Thanksgiving turkey.

SPLIT PEA SOUP

2 cups dried split peas
2 quarts water
1 pound smoked ham shank or ham hocks or 1 ham bone
1 medium onion, finely chopped (about ½ cup)
1 cup finely chopped celery
1 sprig parsley
¼ teaspoon pepper
2 medium carrots, thinly sliced

In large saucepan or Dutch oven, heat peas and water to boiling; boil 2 minutes. Remove from heat; cover and let stand 1 hour.

Add ham shank, onion, celery, parsley and pepper; heat to boiling. Reduce heat; cover and simmer 1½ hours. Add carrots; cover and simmer until carrots are done and soup is of desired consistency, about 30 minutes.

Remove bone; trim meat from bone and add meat to soup. For a thinner consistency, stir milk or water into soup. Season to taste.

Serve half the soup for this meal. Refrigerate remaining soup for the next day. Or pour soup into freezer container and freeze.

2 servings—and 2 for another day.

LETTUCE WEDGES
WITH WALDORF DRESSING

½ cup diced unpared red apple
¼ cup seeded Tokay grape halves
2 tablespoons chopped celery
½ cup blue cheese dressing or mayonnaise
  Lettuce wedges

Mix apple, grapes, celery and dressing; spoon on lettuce wedges.

2 servings.

SPICY RAISIN CAKE

1¼ cups all-purpose flour*
1 cup sugar
1½ teaspoons baking powder
1 teaspoon cinnamon
½ teaspoon salt
½ teaspoon nutmeg
¼ teaspoon cloves
¾ cup milk
⅓ cup shortening
1 egg
1 cup raisins
  Browned Butter Frosting (below)

Heat oven to 350°. Grease and flour baking pan, 8x8x2 or 9x9x2 inches. Into large mixer bowl, measure all ingredients except raisins and frosting. Blend on low speed ½ minute, scraping bowl constantly. Beat on high speed 3 minutes, scraping bowl occasionally. Fold in raisins. Pour into pan. Bake until wooden pick inserted in center comes out clean, 35 to 40 minutes. Cool; frost with Browned Butter Frosting.

*If using self-rising flour, omit baking powder and salt.

Browned Butter Frosting

3 tablespoons butter
1½ cups confectioners' sugar
½ teaspoon vanilla
  About 1 tablespoon milk

In small saucepan, heat butter over medium heat until a delicate brown. Mix into sugar. Stir in vanilla and milk until frosting is smooth and of spreading consistency.

Enough frosting for an 8- or 9-inch square cake.

Variation
Spicy Raisin Cupcakes: Place paper baking cups in 15 or 16 muffin cups. Pour batter into cups, filling each ½ full. Bake 25 to 30 minutes.

Split Pea Soup
Assorted Crackers
Lettuce Wedges with Waldorf Dressing
Spicy Raisin Cake with Browned Butter Frosting

GARLIC-CHIP CHICKEN

¼ cup shortening (part butter) or
   salad oil
I teaspoon garlic salt
⅛ teaspoon pepper
1½ pounds chicken pieces or
   2-pound broiler-fryer chicken,
   quartered
1 bag (3½ ounces) potato chips,
   crushed (about 1½ cups)

Heat oven to 400°. In oven, melt shortening with garlic salt and pepper in baking pan, 9x9x2 inches. Dip chicken into shortening to coat all sides, then roll in potato chips. Place skin side down in pan. Bake uncovered 30 minutes. Turn; bake until thickest pieces are tender, about 30 minutes.

2 servings.

QUICK SCALLOPED POTATOES

Heat oven to 400°. Measure contents of 1 package (5.5 ounces) scalloped potatoes; divide in half (approximately 1 cup potato slices and 3 tablespoons sauce mix).* Place half the potato slices in ungreased 2½-cup or 1-quart casserole. Sprinkle 3 tablespoons sauce mix on slices. Stir in half the amounts of butter, water and milk called for on package. Bake uncovered until potatoes are tender and golden brown, 25 to 30 minutes.

2 generous servings.

*To store remaining mix, close package securely and use within 2 weeks to make Scalloped Potatoes with Ham (page 83).

SKILLET ASPARAGUS

Break off tough ends of ¾ to 1 pound asparagus as far down as stalks snap easily. Wash asparagus and remove scales if sandy or tough. Fill 10-inch skillet ⅓ full with water; add ½ teaspoon salt and heat to boiling. Add asparagus; heat to boiling. Cover and cook until stalk ends are crisp-tender, 8 to 12 minutes. Drain; return asparagus to skillet to dry. Dot with 1 tablespoon butter or margarine.

2 servings.

CRANBERRY RELISH SALAD

1 cup boiling water
1 package (3 ounces) lemon-flavored
   gelatin
1 package (10 ounces) frozen
   cranberry-orange relish
Lettuce

Pour boiling water onto gelatin in bowl; stir until gelatin is dissolved. Stir in frozen relish until thawed. Pour into 4-cup mold or 4 to 6 individual molds. Chill until firm. Place 2 servings on lettuce; if desired, top with mayonnaise. Serve remaining gelatin topped with whipped cream as dessert the next day.

2 servings—and 2 or more for another day.

Note: Pineapple-flavored gelatin can be substituted for the lemon-flavored gelatin. And for variety, add one of the following: 1 can (8¾ ounces) crushed pineapple (with syrup); 1 apple, chopped; ⅓ cup chopped nuts.

BROWNIES À LA MODE

Bake 1 package (15 ounces) fudge brownie mix as directed. For each serving, place scoop of vanilla, coffee or peppermint ice cream on brownie square. Heat ¼ cup chocolate fudge sauce; drizzle on ice cream.

It's a toss-up . . . whether you'll want to liven this easy oven meal with the crisp and crunchy Apple-Celery Toss or the Cabbage Slaw. If time is of the essence, you might note that the slaw can be made ahead and refrigerated.

MUSTARD SHORT RIBS

2 pounds beef short ribs, cut into pieces
2 medium onions, sliced
2 tablespoons prepared mustard
1 tablespoon lemon juice
1 teaspoon sugar
1 teaspoon salt
½ teaspoon instant minced garlic
½ teaspoon pepper

Heat oven to 350°. In 8-inch skillet, brown meat over medium heat. Place meat and onion slices in ungreased 2-quart casserole. Mix remaining ingredients; pour on meat. Cover tightly and bake until meat is tender, about 1½ hours.

2 servings.

BAKED SWEET POTATOES

Heat oven to 350°. Rub 2 medium sweet potatoes with shortening (for soft skins). Prick with fork to allow steam to escape. Bake until tender, about 1 hour.

To serve, cut crisscross gash in each top; squeeze gently until some of potato pops up through opening. Serve with butter or dairy sour cream.

2 servings.

APPLE-CELERY TOSS

1½ cups bite-size pieces lettuce
1 red apple, sliced
¼ cup diagonally sliced celery
¼ cup mayonnaise or oil-and-vinegar dressing

Combine lettuce, apple slices and celery in bowl. Pour mayonnaise on and toss.

2 servings.

CABBAGE SLAW

2 cups coarsely shredded cabbage (about ⅓ head)
¼ cup coarsely chopped unpared cucumber
Dash salt
¼ cup mayonnaise or salad dressing

Combine cabbage, cucumber and salt in bowl. Pour mayonnaise on cabbage mixture and toss.

2 servings.

BUTTERSCOTCH BREAD PUDDING

1 cup soft bread cubes
1 egg
1 tablespoon butter or margarine, melted
⅔ cup milk
3 tablespoons brown sugar
½ teaspoon cinnamon
¼ teaspoon nutmeg
Dash salt
⅓ cup raisins

Heat oven to 350°. Place bread cubes in buttered 2½-cup casserole. Beat egg slightly; stir in butter, milk, brown sugar, seasonings and raisins. Pour egg mixture on bread cubes. Bake until knife inserted halfway between center and edge comes out clean, about 40 minutes. Serve warm. Top with light cream if you like.

2 servings.

Mustard Short Ribs
Baked Sweet Potatoes
Italian Green Beans
Apple-Celery Toss or Cabbage Slaw
Butterscotch Bread Pudding

Looks complicated? Wait—see how easy: While the chicken cooks, stir up the sauce and scoop the sherbet. Prepare the salads except for the dressing and garnish. If you're canny, greens will be already washed and chilled. When the recipe says "Go," add sauce to chicken. Then start the zucchini and spaghetti. Last minute—finish the spinach salads. Indeed, a colorful menu you'll surely decide to repeat . . . again and again.

Chicken Cacciatore
Spaghetti
Zucchini Parmesan
Fresh Spinach Salad
Rainbow Parfaits

CHICKEN CACCIATORE

    Salad oil
¼ cup all-purpose flour
½ teaspoon salt
⅛ teaspoon pepper
⅛ teaspoon paprika
1 to 1½ pounds chicken pieces or 2-pound broiler-fryer chicken, cut up
1 jar (15 ounces) meatless spaghetti sauce
1 can (2 ounces) mushroom stems and pieces
¼ teaspoon instant minced garlic
1 teaspoon parsley flakes
¼ cup sliced pitted ripe olives
3½ to 4 ounces uncooked spaghetti

Heat ⅛ inch salad oil in large skillet. Mix flour, salt, pepper and paprika; coat chicken with flour mixture. Cook chicken in oil over medium heat until light brown, 15 to 20 minutes. Mix spaghetti sauce, mushrooms (with liquid), garlic, parsley flakes and olives. Drain fat from skillet. Pour sauce onto chicken. Heat to boiling. Reduce heat; cover tightly and simmer until thickest pieces of chicken are tender, about 30 minutes.

While chicken simmers, cook spaghetti as directed on package. Drain. Serve chicken with spaghetti.

2 servings.

ZUCCHINI PARMESAN

Cut 1 medium zucchini into strips, 2x½ inch. Heat 1 inch salted water (½ teaspoon salt to 1 cup water) to boiling. Add zucchini. Cover and heat to boiling; cook until tender, 7 to 9 minutes. Drain. Add 1 tablespoon butter or margarine and toss. Sprinkle 1 tablespoon grated Parmesan cheese on zucchini.

2 servings.

FRESH SPINACH SALAD

2 cups bite-size pieces spinach leaves (about 5 ounces)
2 green onions, sliced
    Seasoned salt
2 tablespoons imitation bacon
2 tablespoons oil-and-vinegar dressing

Divide spinach between salad bowls. Sprinkle onion slices, seasoned salt and imitation bacon on spinach. Drizzle 1 tablespoon dressing on each serving. If you like, garnish with lemon twists.

2 servings.

RAINBOW PARFAITS

Choose 2 or 3 flavors sherbet, such as raspberry, pineapple and/or lime (about ½ pint each). Make balls with scoop or spoon. Divide between parfait glasses and place in freezer.

At serving time, fill glasses with ginger ale, and if desired, garnish each with whipped topping.

2 servings.

Put your creative foot forward with a menu that's undull all the way . . . from the deliciously sauced chicken to the rainbowed dessert. Beautiful? Indeed! Best of all, it's suited to the barest of budgets. Be sure to remember this dessert when the high cost of entertaining gets you down. The recipe is meant for two, of course—but all you have to do is double up.

DIXIE BAKE WITH BUTTERMILK BISCUITS

1 can (12 ounces) pork luncheon
   meat
12 whole cloves
¼ cup apricot preserves
1 teaspoon water
¼ teaspoon dry mustard
1 cup buttermilk baking mix
¼ cup water

Heat oven to 425°. Score top of meat, cutting 12 squares or diamonds 1 inch deep. Insert clove in each square. Place meat in ungreased baking pan, 8x8x2 inches, pushing meat to one side of pan. Mix preserves, 1 teaspoon water and the mustard; spoon on meat.

Stir baking mix and ¼ cup water with fork to a soft dough. Turn onto floured cloth-covered board; smooth dough into ball and knead 5 times. Roll dough ½ inch thick. Cut into five 2-inch biscuits; place in pan with meat. Bake until biscuits are golden brown and meat is hot, 15 to 20 minutes.

2 servings.

Time-saver: Forget all about kneading and rolling the dough. Instead, drop by spoonfuls (5) right into the pan.

Something to Know About...

Pork luncheon meat can be scored to form diamonds, as shown here, or squares. Insert a clove in each diamond to make something simple look like something special.

SUCCOTASH

½ package (10-ounce size) frozen
   corn and lima beans
¼ teaspoon salt
   Dash pepper
2 tablespoons light cream
1 tablespoon butter or margarine

Cook corn and lima beans as directed except—use only half the amounts of water and salt called for on package. Drain. Add remaining ingredients; heat, stirring occasionally, until butter is melted.

2 servings.

CRANBERRY-PINEAPPLE SALAD

1 can (8 ounces) jellied cranberry
   sauce, cut into ¼-inch slices
1 can (8½ ounces) sliced pineapple,
   drained
   Crisp salad greens

Arrange cranberry and pineapple slices on salad greens. Serve with mayonnaise or salad dressing if you like.

2 servings.

Variation

Cranberry-Orange Salad: Substitute 1 orange, pared and cut into ¼-inch slices, for the pineapple.

CHOCOLATE-CINNAMON ICE CREAM

Soften 1 pint chocolate ice cream slightly; stir in ½ teaspoon cinnamon. Spoon ice cream into original container, refrigerator tray or dessert dishes and freeze until firm.

2 servings.

Riddle: How do you turn *hot* chili into a frozen asset? Easy. Simply double the recipe and stash half in the freezer as a head start for another meal. There's time, while the chili cooks, to turn out the butter sticks, toss the salad and stir up the pudding dessert. Then for a quick chill, pop the dessert dishes in the freezer until ready to serve. All set? Turn on a South-of-the-Border record to give your dinner an appropriate accent.

CHILI CON CARNE

½ pound ground beef
1 medium onion, chopped (about ½ cup)
½ cup chopped green pepper
1 can (16 ounces) tomatoes
1 can (8 ounces) tomato sauce
1 teaspoon salt
1 to 2 teaspoons chili powder
Dash cayenne red pepper
Dash paprika
1 can (8 ounces) kidney beans

In 8-inch skillet, cook and stir meat, onion and green pepper until meat is brown and onion is tender. Drain off fat. Stir in remaining ingredients except beans. Heat to boiling. Reduce heat; cook uncovered about 30 minutes. Stir in beans (with liquid); heat until bubbly.

2 servings.

CUCUMBER-ICEBERG SALAD

1½ cups shredded iceberg lettuce
½ medium cucumber, cut into cubes
Grated Parmesan cheese
Oil-and-vinegar dressing

Toss lettuce and cucumber cubes in bowl; sprinkle cheese on top. Serve with dressing.

2 servings.

CORNMEAL BUTTER STICKS

¼ cup butter or margarine
½ cup buttermilk baking mix
½ cup cornmeal
¼ cup water
Salt

Heat oven to 450°. In oven, melt butter in baking pan, 9x9x2 inches. Stir baking mix, cornmeal and water with fork to soft dough. Turn onto floured cloth-covered board; smooth dough into ball and knead 5 times. Roll into rectangle, 6x4 inches. Cut into 8 strips, 4x¾ inch.

Dip each strip into melted butter, coating all sides, and arrange in pan. Sprinkle salt lightly on strips. Bake until golden brown, 12 to 15 minutes. Serve hot.

8 sticks.

PINEAPPLE PUDDING

1 can (8¼ ounces) crushed pineapple, drained
½ can (17.5-ounce size) vanilla pudding (1 cup)
Toasted coconut

Fold pineapple into pudding; divide between dessert dishes. Chill. Top each serving with coconut.

2 servings.

Chili con Carne
Cucumber-Iceberg Salad
Ripe Olives
Cornmeal Butter Sticks
Pineapple Pudding

Sometimes the very simplest of meals is the most memorable. Especially one with such pungent, old-world fragrance and hearty goodness. All this and "cents-ible" besides! After the robust main dish, you'll like the contrast of a light, refreshing dessert, just tweaked with spicy overtones.

SAUSAGE AND SAUERKRAUT WITH DUMPLINGS

1 can (8 ounces) sauerkraut
4 medium Polish or bratwurst
   sausages
¼ teaspoon caraway seed
1 tablespoon chopped onion
½ cup water
½ cup buttermilk baking mix
3 tablespoons milk
   Snipped parsley

In saucepan, heat sauerkraut (with liquid), sausages, caraway seed, onion and water to boiling. Reduce heat; cover and simmer 30 minutes.

Stir baking mix and milk with fork to a soft dough. Drop dough by spoonfuls (2 or 3) onto sauerkraut. Cook uncovered over low heat 10 minutes; cover and cook 10 minutes. Remove dumplings, sausages and sauerkraut with slotted spoon to serving platter. Garnish with parsley.

2 servings.

FRESH VEGETABLE RELISHES

Arrange a variety of vegetables attractively on small tray or in mug. Suggestions include: cherry tomatoes; carrot, cucumber, celery or zucchini sticks; green or red pepper strips or rings. Or prepare any of the vegetable relishes below. Chill until serving time.

Broccoli Buds and Cauliflowerets: Break head of broccoli or cauliflower into bite-size flowerets.

Carrot Curls: With vegetable parer, cut carrot lengthwise into paper-thin slices. Roll up slices and fasten with picks. Place in ice and water. (Remove picks before serving.)

Cucumber Petals: Run tines of fork down length of unpared cucumber. Cut crosswise into very thin slices.

Green Onions: Remove any loose layers of skin. Trim, leaving about 3 inches of green.

Radish Fans: Remove stem and root ends from large radishes. Make thin crosswise cuts almost through radishes. Place in ice and water.

Rutabaga or Turnip Strips: Thinly pare raw rutabaga or turnip; cut into narrow strips or thin slices. For an attractive design, use a lattice cutter.

SPICED APPLESAUCE À LA MODE

1 cup applesauce
½ teaspoon cinnamon
½ teaspoon lemon juice
   Vanilla ice cream

In small saucepan, heat applesauce, cinnamon and lemon juice, stirring occasionally, until hot. Divide applesauce between dessert dishes. Top each serving with ice cream.

2 servings.

When you're trying to trim your food budget, it's wise to remember that the more economical cuts of meat have just as much protein as the more expensive cuts.

Think about ground beef and stew meat for budget savings on beef. You can buy stew meat ready-cut, or you can cut it yourself from blade steak or bottom round. Round steak, you'll find, is also econom-ical because it has little or no bone or fat. (Top round is usually more ten-der than bottom round.)

Keep a sharp eye out for supermarket specials—even if they're meant as big-family buys. For ex-ample, a little imagination and a 3- to 4-pound arm pot roast can take care of 3 meals. Cut the round end into stew meat, use the center part for a pot roast and slice the re-mainder horizontally into 2 pieces of Swiss steak.

With pork, the first- and the end-cut chops are your best buy; they are as tender and tasty as the center chops but cost less. For the same reason, choose shoulder chops of lamb rather than loin or rib chops.

Don't forget liver, tongue and kidney; they are very nutritious and reasonably priced.

Something Special...

Budget Meat Buys

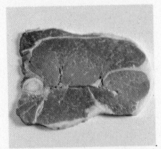

Round steak: Use in South-western Beef, Swiss Steak, Mexican Steak 'n Beans, Viennese Steak or Curried Beef and Peppers.

Beef short ribs: Use in Mustard Short Ribs. Beef stew meat: Use in Savory Beef Stew.

Blade steak: Use in Bar-becued Chuck Steak. Cubed steaks: Use in Steak Stroganoff or Minute Steaks with Butter Sauce.

Smoked ham hocks: Use in Split Pea Soup. Polish sausage: Use in Sausage and Sauerkraut with Dump-lings.

Spareribs: Use in Sweet-and-Sour Ribs. Pork loin chops: Use in Orange Pork Chop Skillet or Lemon Bar-becued Pork Chops.

Lamb shanks: Use in Braised Lamb Shanks and Vegetables. Lamb shoulder chops: Use in Herbed Lamb Chops.

Hot dog! To a certain generation, that meant "wow." It still does when applied to this hefty hot salad and franks.

FRANKFURTERS

Drop 4 large frankfurters (about ¾ pound) into boiling water. Cover; reduce heat and simmer until heated through, 5 to 8 minutes. Remove frankfurters from water with tongs.

2 servings.

HOT GERMAN POTATO SALAD

2 medium potatoes, pared and halved
3 slices bacon
⅓ cup chopped onion
1 tablespoon flour
2 teaspoons sugar
¾ teaspoon salt
¼ teaspoon celery seed
Dash pepper
⅓ cup water
3 tablespoons vinegar

Heat 1 inch salted water (½ teaspoon salt to 1 cup water) to boiling. Add potatoes. Cover and heat to boiling; cook until tender, 20 to 25 minutes. Drain and set aside.

In 8-inch skillet, fry bacon until crisp; remove and drain. In same skillet, cook and stir onion in bacon fat until tender. Stir in flour, sugar, salt, celery seed and pepper. Cook over low heat, stirring until mixture is bubbly. Remove from heat. Stir in water and vinegar. Heat to boiling, stirring constantly. Boil and stir 1 minute. Remove from heat.

Crumble bacon into hot mixture, then slice warm potatoes into hot mixture. Cook until hot and bubbly, stirring lightly to coat potato slices.

2 servings.

BUTTERED GREEN BEANS

Cook ½ package (9-ounce size) frozen cut green beans as directed except—use only half the amounts of water and salt called for on package. Drain. Dot with 1 tablespoon butter or margarine and sprinkle with chopped salted peanuts, sunflower seeds or almonds.

2 servings.

CHERRY SKILLET COBBLER

½ can (21-ounce size) cherry pie filling*
¼ cup orange juice
½ cup buttermilk baking mix
1 tablespoon shredded orange peel, if desired
1½ teaspoons sugar
2 tablespoons milk

In 1-quart saucepan, heat pie filling and orange juice to boiling, stirring occasionally. Stir baking mix, orange peel, sugar and milk with fork to a soft dough. Drop dough by spoonfuls (2 or 3) onto boiling cherry mixture. Cook uncovered over low heat 10 minutes; cover and cook 10 minutes longer. Serve warm. Top with light cream or ice cream if you wish.

2 servings.

*Leftover pie filling? Use for dessert later in the week. Spoon over vanilla ice cream, pound cake or brownies.

Here's a dinner with an air of "Home on the Range" about it. Plus a choice of do-ahead desserts: one a speedy spin-off on a Continental flan, the other strictly U.S.A.

SOUTHWESTERN BEEF

¾- to 1-pound beef round steak,
   1 to 2 inches thick
2 cloves garlic, thinly sliced
1 tablespoon salad oil
½ teaspoon salt
   Dash marjoram or basil
¼ cup water
1 tablespoon butter or margarine
⅓ cup raisins
1 large or 2 small tomatoes, peeled
   and cut into wedges
   Pickled chili peppers

Cut about 10 small slits in meat with tip of knife; insert a garlic slice in each. Heat oil in 8-inch skillet; brown meat over medium heat, about 15 minutes. Drain off fat. Add salt, marjoram and water; heat to boiling. Reduce heat; cover tightly and simmer until tender, 1 to 1½ hours. (Add small amount of water if necessary.)

Melt butter in small saucepan. Add raisins and tomatoes; cook over low heat, stirring occasionally, until hot, about 5 minutes. Pour around steak and garnish with chili peppers.

2 servings.

Time-saver: Use ¾-pound beef round steak, ½ inch thick, and omit garlic slices. After browning meat, add salt, marjoram and water; cover and simmer until tender, about 45 minutes.

TANGY CAULIFLOWER SALAD

½ medium cauliflower
2 tablespoons oil-and-vinegar
   dressing
¼ teaspoon oregano
¼ teaspoon salt
   Lettuce leaves

Separate cauliflower into flowerets. Heat 1 inch salted water (½ teaspoon salt to 1 cup water) to boiling. Add cauliflower. Cover and heat to boiling; cook until tender, 10 to 12 minutes. Drain.

Mix dressing, oregano and salt; pour on hot cauliflower and toss. Cover and refrigerate at least 3 hours.

To serve, remove cauliflower with slotted spoon to lettuce-lined bowls. Garnish with finely chopped green onion or grated Parmesan cheese and parsley.

2 servings.

Time-saver: Substitute 1 package (10 ounces) frozen cauliflower, cooked as directed, for the fresh.

QUICK CORN MUFFINS

Measure 1 package (14 ounces) corn muffin mix; divide in half (approximately 1½ cups).* Prepare muffins as directed except —use half the mix, 1 egg and half the amount of milk called for on package.

6 muffins.

*To store remaining mix, close package securely and use within 3 weeks to make hot muffins for another meal. Or if you prefer, prepare entire package and freeze leftover muffins to use as needed.

CARAMEL CUSTARD

1 egg, slightly beaten
2 tablespoons sugar
   Dash salt
½ teaspoon vanilla
¾ cup milk, scalded
2 tablespoons caramel ice-cream
   topping

Heat oven to 350°. Mix egg, sugar, salt and vanilla. Stir in milk. Place 1 tablespoon caramel topping in each of two 6-ounce custard cups. Pour egg mixture onto caramel topping.

Place cups in baking pan, 8x8x2 inches; pour very hot water into pan to within ½ inch of tops of cups. Bake until knife inserted halfway between center and edge comes out clean, 40 to 45 minutes. Remove cups from water; serve warm or chill and unmold into dessert dishes.

2 servings.

FROSTY PUMPKIN CUSTARD

Line 6 muffin cups with paper baking cups. Soften ½ pint vanilla ice cream slightly. Fold ½ can (16-ounce size) pumpkin pie mix* into ice cream. Divide among paper-lined cups. Cover and freeze until firm, at least 3 hours. Garnish with whipped topping and walnut halves.

2 servings—and 4 for other days.

*Leftover pumpkin pie mix? Use in Pumpkin Custards (page 89).

Think Mardi Gras to cure a case of the "Mondays." Your kitchen takes on a French Quarter air with the heady aroma of spicy shrimp simmering in a cook-and-serve skillet. But it wouldn't be a New Orleans dinner without French onion soup; even a quickie from a can can be oo-la-la if you add your own small touch of genius: a thin slice of toasted French bread in each soup bowl, a sprinkle of grated Parmesan cheese on top.

French Onion Soup
Shrimp Creole
Fluffy White Rice
Tossed Green Salad
French Bread
Southern Ambrosia
Praline Squares

SHRIMP CREOLE

    2 tablespoons butter or margarine
    ¾ cup chopped onion
    ½ cup chopped celery
    1 medium green pepper, chopped
       (about ½ cup)
    1 small clove garlic, minced,
       or ⅛ teaspoon instant minced
       garlic
    1 can (8 ounces) tomato sauce
    ½ cup water
    1 teaspoon parsley flakes or
       snipped parsley
    ½ teaspoon salt
    ⅛ teaspoon cayenne red pepper
    1 bay leaf, crushed
    1 package (7 ounces) frozen
       cleaned raw shrimp* (about
       1 cup)
    1½ cups hot cooked rice

Melt butter in 8-inch skillet; cook and stir onion, celery, green pepper and garlic over medium heat until onion is tender. Stir in tomato sauce, water, parsley flakes and seasonings. Simmer uncovered 20 minutes, stirring occasionally. Stir in frozen shrimp; heat to boiling. Reduce heat; cover and simmer until shrimp are done, about 10 minutes. Serve on rice.

2 servings.

*Rinse frozen shrimp under running cold water to remove ice glaze before adding to sauce.

SOUTHERN AMBROSIA

Sprinkle confectioners' sugar and flaked coconut on orange slices.

PRALINE SQUARES

    ¼ cup shortening or salad oil
    1 cup brown sugar (packed)
    1 egg
    1 teaspoon vanilla
    ¾ cup all-purpose flour*
    1 teaspoon baking powder
    ½ teaspoon salt
    ½ cup chopped nuts

Heat oven to 350°. Grease baking pan, 8x8x2 inches. Melt shortening in saucepan over low heat. Remove from heat; mix in sugar, egg and vanilla. Stir in remaining ingredients. Spread in pan. Bake 25 minutes. While warm, cut into 2-inch squares.

16 squares.

*If using self-rising flour, omit baking powder and salt.

Something to Know About...

No matter what part of the country you live in, no matter what time of year it is, you can always find shrimp in one form or another.

Raw shrimp in the shell, sometimes called green shrimp, can be purchased fresh or frozen. They're also available shelled and deveined. Or you can buy shrimp that are already cleaned and cooked—canned or frozen in packages.

For every 1 cup cleaned cooked shrimp your recipe calls for, you can

☐ prepare 1 package (7 ounces) frozen peeled shrimp or . . .

☐ prepare ¾ pound fresh or frozen raw shrimp (in shells) or . . .

☐ use 1 can (4½ or 5 ounces) shrimp.

Crisp, crusty fried chicken that really isn't fried at all. It's baked—just like the one pictured on page 49. No tiresome tending and, best of all, no spattering. And since the shortcakes bake at the same temperature, they can share the oven toward the end. Now, that's teamwork.

OVEN-FRIED CHICKEN

¼ cup shortening (part butter) or salad oil
¼ cup all-purpose flour
½ teaspoon salt
⅛ teaspoon paprika
⅛ teaspoon pepper
1½ pounds chicken pieces or 2-pound broiler-fryer chicken, cut into quarters

Heat oven to 425°. In oven, melt shortening in baking pan, 9x9x2 inches or 11¾x7½x1½ inches. Mix flour, salt, paprika and pepper in plastic or paper bag; shake chicken, 2 or 3 pieces at a time, in bag until coated.

Place chicken skin side down in pan. Bake uncovered 30 minutes. Turn chicken; bake until tender, 15 to 20 minutes longer.

2 servings.

PARSLEYED NEW POTATOES

1 pound new potatoes (6 to 8 small)
2 tablespoons butter or margarine
1 to 2 tablespoons snipped parsley

Scrub unpared potatoes lightly with vegetable brush. Heat 1 inch salted water (1 teaspoon salt to 1 cup water) to boiling. Add potatoes. Cover and heat to boiling; cook until tender, 20 to 25 minutes. Drain. Add butter; toss until potatoes are coated. Sprinkle with parsley.

2 servings.

ASPARAGUS ALMONDINE

1 package (10 ounces) frozen asparagus spears
1 tablespoon butter or margarine
2 tablespoons diced roasted almonds

Cook asparagus spears as directed on package. Drain. Turn into serving dish; dot with butter and sprinkle almonds on top.

2 servings.

STRAWBERRY SHORTCAKE

1 pint fresh strawberries
⅓ to ½ cup sugar
1 cup buttermilk baking mix
¼ cup milk
1 tablespoon sugar
1 tablespoon butter or margarine, melted

Slice strawberries into bowl. Sprinkle ⅓ to ½ cup sugar on berries and let stand about 1 hour.

Heat oven to 425°. Mix remaining ingredients with fork to a soft dough. Turn dough onto lightly floured cloth-covered board; smooth dough into ball and knead 8 to 10 times. Roll ½ inch thick. Cut into two 3-inch circles. Place on ungreased baking sheet. Bake 10 to 12 minutes.

Split warm shortcakes; spoon strawberries between layers and on top. Serve with sweetened whipped cream if desired.

2 servings.

Variation
Peach-Praline Shortcake: Omit strawberries and sugar. Before baking, brush soft butter or margarine on circles; sprinkle brown sugar on tops. Fill and top shortcakes with sweetened sliced peaches.

**Oven-fried Chicken
Parsleyed New Potatoes
Asparagus Almondine
Crisp Vegetable Relishes
Strawberry Shortcake**

To make a perfect puffy omelet, gently fold the egg yolk mixture into the stiffly beaten egg whites with a rubber scraper. Don't overfold, or you'll deflate the mixture.

Cook the omelet on top of the range until it's puffy and the bottom is light brown, lift the edge to judge the color. It then goes into the oven to bake until it's done.

Fill the omelet with part of the sauce. Tip the skillet and fold the omelet in half. Slide it onto a platter and pour the remaining sauce on top.

PUFFY OMELET CAHUENGA

Puffy Omelet (below)
1 ripe small avocado
¾ cup dairy sour cream
½ teaspoon salt
⅛ teaspoon dill weed
1 large tomato, peeled, diced
  and drained

Prepare Puffy Omelet. While omelet bakes, peel and dice avocado. Heat sour cream, salt and dill weed (do not boil). Gently stir tomato and avocado into sour cream mixture; heat through.

To serve, pour part of the sauce on omelet in skillet. Tip skillet and loosen omelet by slipping rubber scraper, pancake turner or spatula under; fold omelet and remove to heated platter. Pour remaining sauce on top.

2 generous servings.

Puffy Omelet

3 eggs, separated
3 tablespoons milk or water
¼ teaspoon salt
⅛ teaspoon pepper
1 tablespoon butter or
  margarine

In small mixer bowl, beat egg whites until stiff but not dry. Beat egg yolks until thick and lemon colored. Beat in milk, salt and pepper; gently fold into egg whites with rubber scraper.

Heat oven to 325°. In 8-inch skillet with ovenproof handle, heat butter until just hot enough to sizzle a drop of water, rotating skillet so that butter evenly coats the bottom. Pour omelet mixture into skillet; level surface gently. Reduce heat; cook until puffy and light brown on bottom, about 5 minutes. (Lift omelet at edge to judge color.)

Place skillet in oven; bake until knife inserted in center comes out clean, 12 to 15 minutes.

MAPLE-GLAZED BACON

½ pound Canadian-style bacon,
  cut into ¼-inch slices
2 tablespoons maple-flavored
  syrup

Heat oven to 325°. In ungreased small shallow baking dish, overlap bacon slices slightly. Drizzle syrup on slices. Bake uncovered until bacon is hot, about 35 minutes.

2 servings.

MARINATED GREEN BEAN SALAD

Drain liquid from 1 can (8 ounces) French-style green beans. Pour 2 tablespoons Italian dressing on beans. Cover and refrigerate at least 2 hours. Drain. Serve beans on crisp salad greens and garnish with onion rings.

2 servings.

FRESH FRUIT CUP

Choose two or more of the following fruits to total 1 to 1½ cups: banana slices; blueberries; strawberries; raspberries; seedless green grapes; peach, pear or pineapple chunks; orange or grapefruit sections or melon cubes. Divide between dessert dishes and top each with ¼ cup orange juice or ginger ale.

2 servings.

Puffy Omelet Cahuenga
Maple-glazed Bacon
Marinated Green Bean Salad
Toasted English Muffins
Fresh Fruit Cup

MEAT LOAF

1 egg
½ cup milk
⅓ cup dry bread crumbs or 1 cup soft bread crumbs (about 1½ slices bread, torn into small pieces)
1 pound ground beef or meat loaf mixture
2 tablespoons finely chopped onion
½ teaspoon salt
⅛ teaspoon pepper
¼ teaspoon dry mustard
¼ teaspoon garlic salt
1 teaspoon Worcestershire sauce

Mix all ingredients thoroughly. Divide meat mixture in half (about 1½ cups each); shape each into loaf, 5x4 inches. Place both loaves in ungreased loaf pan, 9x5x3 inches, or baking pan, 9x9x2 inches.

Bake in 350° oven about 45 minutes. If desired, top one loaf with catsup, chili sauce or strips of cheese and return to oven for 2 to 3 minutes. Serve this loaf immediately. Cool remaining loaf; wrap in aluminum foil, label and freeze.

2 servings—and 2 for another time.

Variation

Mini Meat Loaves: Divide meat mixture into 4 equal parts (about ¾ cup each). Spread each in ungreased miniature loaf pan, 4½x2½x1½ inches, or shape into individual loaves and place in ungreased baking pan, 9x9x2 inches. Bake about 35 minutes. Serve 2 loaves immediately. Cool remaining loaves; wrap in aluminum foil, label and freeze.

Note: To serve frozen meat loaf, place foil-wrapped *frozen* loaf or miniloaves on oven rack; heat in 350° oven 50 to 60 minutes.

CREAMY SCALLOPED POTATOES

2 tablespoons butter or margarine
2 tablespoons flour
½ teaspoon salt
⅛ teaspoon pepper
1½ cups milk
1 pound potatoes (about 3 medium), pared and thinly sliced
2 tablespoons finely chopped onion
1 teaspoon butter or margarine

Heat oven to 350°. Melt 2 tablespoons butter over low heat. Stir in flour and seasonings. Cook over low heat, stirring until smooth and bubbly. Remove from heat. Stir in milk. Heat to boiling, stirring constantly.

In greased 1-quart casserole, layer half the potatoes, all the onion and half the sauce. Top with remaining potatoes and sauce. Dot with 1 teaspoon butter.

Cover and bake 30 minutes. Uncover and bake until potatoes are tender, about 35 minutes.

2 servings.

PEACH CRISPS

4 canned peach halves, drained
2 tablespoons chopped walnuts
2 tablespoons brown sugar
1½ teaspoons finely shredded orange peel
⅛ teaspoon allspice
4 walnut halves

Heat oven to 350°. Place peach halves cut sides up in ungreased baking dish. Mix chopped walnuts, sugar, orange peel and allspice; sprinkle on peaches. Bake until hot, about 20 minutes. Serve warm; top each with walnut half and, if desired, vanilla ice cream.

2 servings.

Time for a change? The meat loaf mix on page 56 can be a whole new "ball" game if you fix half loaf, half meatballs. (Either will keep frozen up to 2 months.) Note the change in procedure, too. These meatballs bake in the oven—no watching, no stirring, no spattering.

BAKED MEATBALLS

Prepare mixture for Meat Loaf (page 56) except—decrease milk to ¼ cup. Shape mixture into twenty 1½-inch balls. Place in ungreased baking pan, 9x9x2 inches. Bake in 400° oven about 20 minutes. Serve half the meatballs immediately. Cool remaining meatballs; place in 1-pint freezer container, label and freeze.

2 servings—and 2 for another day.

Note: To serve frozen meatballs, heat 1 jar (about 15 ounces) favorite spaghetti sauce in 1-quart saucepan to boiling; add frozen meatballs. Reduce heat; cover and simmer until meatballs are hot, about 20 minutes. Serve with hot cooked spaghetti or noodles. Or heat 1 can (10¾ ounces) beef gravy to boiling; add frozen meatballs and heat through. Serve with mashed potatoes.

OVEN RICE

1 cup boiling water
½ cup uncooked regular rice
½ teaspoon salt
  Snipped parsley

Heat oven to 400°. Mix water, rice and salt in ungreased 2½-cup or 1-quart casserole. Cover tightly; bake until liquid is absorbed and rice is tender, 20 to 25 minutes. Sprinkle parsley on top.

1½ cups rice.

SPANISH PEPPERS

1 to 1½ green peppers, cut into
  ½-inch strips
½ cup ¼-inch diagonal slices
  celery
2 tablespoons finely chopped
  onion
1 tablespoon salad oil
¼ teaspoon basil leaves
½ teaspoon salt
  Dash pepper
1 can (8 ounces) tomato sauce

In 8-inch skillet, cook and stir green pepper, celery and onion in oil over medium heat until onion is tender. Stir in remaining ingredients. Cover and cook over medium heat until green pepper is crisp-tender, about 5 minutes.

2 servings.

QUICK BLUEBERRY COBBLER

½ can (21-ounce size) blueberry pie
  filling*
½ teaspoon shredded orange peel
½ cup buttermilk baking mix
2 teaspoons sugar
2 tablespoons orange juice
2 teaspoons butter or margarine,
  softened

Heat oven to 400°. Mix pie filling and orange peel in ungreased 2½-cup casserole. Heat in oven 15 minutes. Stir baking mix, sugar, orange juice and butter with fork to soft dough. Drop dough by spoonfuls (2 or 3) onto hot blueberry mixture. Bake until topping is light brown, 15 to 20 minutes. Serve warm, with light cream or ice cream if you like.

2 servings.

*Leftover pie filling? Serve in tart shells or use as a topping for vanilla ice cream, lemon sherbet, vanilla pudding, pancakes or French toast.

Baked Meatballs
Oven Rice
Spanish Peppers
Cabbage Slaw (page 41)
Quick Blueberry Cobbler

If you both agree that "It's too nice to eat in," take that as your cue to cook out—in style. Try ham steak sporting a splendid glaze, and surprise packets of vegetable, muffins and dessert for a note of mystery. The coals for cooking should be gray on the outside, glowing on the inside and medium hot. That's about 350° on a grill thermometer, or as hot as your hand can stand when held near (not on!) the grid for 3 to 4 seconds.

HEARTY HAM STEAK

2 tablespoons prepared mustard
2 tablespoons pineapple juice or
    other fruit juice
1 tablespoon brown sugar
1 teaspoon horseradish
    Dash salt
1 fully cooked ham slice, about
    ¾ inch thick

Combine all ingredients except ham slice in small saucepan; heat to boiling, stirring occasionally.

Place ham on grill 4 inches from medium coals. Cook until hot and glazed, about 5 minutes on each side, basting frequently with mustard mixture.

2 servings.

GRILLED SWEET POTATOES

Pare 2 sweet potatoes; cut diagonally into ½-inch slices. Cook slices in 1 inch boiling water 10 minutes. Drain. Mix 2 tablespoons butter or margarine, melted, and ¼ teaspoon salt.

Place potato slices on grill 4 inches from medium coals. Cook 10 minutes on each side, brushing frequently with butter mixture. Sprinkle toasted coconut on potato slices.

2 servings.

PEAS ALMONDINE IN FOIL

1 package (10 ounces) frozen
    green peas
2 tablespoons slivered almonds
    Salt and pepper
1 tablespoon butter or margarine
1 teaspoon chopped pimiento, if
    desired

Place frozen block of peas on 18-inch square of double thickness heavy-duty aluminum foil. Sprinkle almonds, salt and pepper on peas. Dot with butter. Wrap securely in foil. Cook directly on medium coals, turning once, until tender, 18 to 20 minutes. Add pimiento just before serving.

2 servings.

CORN MUFFINS FROM THE GRILL

Bake Quick Corn Muffins (page 51) ahead of time. Split and butter each muffin. Wrap in double thickness heavy-duty aluminum foil. Heat on grill 4 inches from medium coals until hot, about 10 minutes, turning once.

BANANA BOATS

For each serving, cut V-shaped wedge lengthwise in a peeled firm banana. Place on piece of double thickness heavy-duty aluminum foil, 18x6 inches. Fill groove in banana with miniature or cut-up marshmallows and chocolate pieces. Wrap tightly in foil. Cook directly on medium coals about 10 minutes.

To grate lemon or orange peel: Rub fruit on fine part of grater, using short strokes. Grate only outer colored part of peel.

To cut julienne strips: Cut meat or vegetables into narrow lengthwise strips.

To snip parsley: Cut or break off stems. Place sprigs in glass measuring cup and snip with kitchen shears.

To coat chicken, meat or vegetables: Place flour or crumbs in plastic or paper bag. Shake a few pieces at a time.

To peel tomatoes: Dip in boiling water 1 minute. Plunge into cold water. Skin will peel off easily.

To chop nuts, vegetables or fruits: Hold down point of French knife and rock blade vertically by handle, swiveling from side to side.

To slice mushrooms: Trim off spots; cut off ends of stems. Slice whole mushrooms through stems.

To slice celery or other vegetables: Cut into thin slices on the diagonal for pretty salads and Oriental specialties.

To dice onion: Peel. Cut off end slice; cut exposed surface deeply into squares. Cut crosswise into slices, making ¼-inch cubes.

Something Special...

Kitchen Know-How

SWISS STEAK

¾-pound beef round steak,
  ½ to ¾ inch thick
2 tablespoons flour
¼ teaspoon salt
⅛ teaspoon pepper
2 tablespoons salad oil
1 can (8 ounces) stewed
  tomatoes
1 medium green pepper,
  sliced
1 medium onion, sliced
½ teaspoon salt

Cut meat into 2 pieces. Mix flour, ¼ teaspoon salt and the pepper; coat meat with flour mixture. Heat oil in 8-inch skillet; brown meat over medium heat, about 15 minutes. Add tomatoes to skillet. Reduce heat; cover and simmer 30 minutes. Add green pepper, onion and ½ teaspoon salt. Cover and simmer until meat is tender, 30 to 45 minutes. (Add small amount water if necessary.)

2 servings.

APPLE-GRAPEFRUIT SALAD

Arrange unpared red apple slices and grapefruit sections on salad greens. Serve with Lime-Honey Dressing (below).

Lime-Honey Dressing

3 tablespoons frozen limeade
  or lemonade concentrate
  (thawed)*
3 tablespoons honey
3 tablespoons salad oil or
  dairy sour cream
¼ teaspoon celery seed

Beat all ingredients until well blended.

½ cup.

*Leftover concentrate? Use in Lime Frappé (page 12) or Fresh Fruit Salad (page 72), drizzle it over a fruit cup or stir up a quick fruit drink.

PECAN TARTS

½ stick pie crust mix
1 egg
¼ cup sugar
⅛ teaspoon salt
3 tablespoons butter or margarine,
  melted
⅓ cup dark corn syrup
⅓ cup pecan halves or pieces

Heat oven to 375°. Prepare pastry for One-crust Pie as directed except—use only half the amount of water called for on package and divide dough in half. Roll each half 1 inch larger than 4-inch tart pan. Ease into pan; flute edge. (Do not prick.)

In small mixer bowl, beat egg, sugar, salt, butter and syrup. Stir in nuts. Pour into pastry-lined tart pans. Bake until filling is set and pastry is light brown, 30 to 35 minutes. Serve warm or cool. Top with whipped cream if desired.

2 tarts.

No 4-inch tart pans? Use 1 stick or ½ packet pie crust mix. Prepare pastry for One-crust Pie as directed on package except—divide dough into 6 equal parts. Shape each into a ball and roll into 4½-inch circle. Ease into muffin cup or 6-ounce custard cup, making pleats so pastry will fit closely. (Do not prick.) Pour filling into pastry-lined muffin cups. Bake about 30 minutes.

CANADIAN-STYLE BACON

Place four to six ⅛-inch slices Canadian-style bacon (about ⅓ pound) in cold skillet. Cook over low heat, turning to brown evenly on both sides, 8 to 10 minutes.

2 servings.

OVEN-BAKED BEANS

2 slices bacon, diced
1 small onion, sliced
1 can (16 ounces) baked beans
   with pork
2 tablespoons catsup or chili sauce
2 tablespoons brown sugar, if
   desired
1 teaspoon Worcestershire sauce
½ teaspoon prepared mustard

Heat oven to 350°. In large skillet, cook and stir bacon and onion until bacon is crisp. Drain off fat. Stir in remaining ingredients. Pour into ungreased 1-quart casserole. Bake uncovered until hot and bubbly, about 45 minutes.

2 servings.

MIXED VEGETABLE SALAD

½ to 1 cup sliced or diced
   vegetables
   Oil-and-Vinegar Dressing (page 62)
   or 3 tablespoons Italian dressing
1 to 1½ cups bite-size pieces crisp
   salad greens

Marinate vegetables in dressing 1 to 2 hours. (Here are a few for-instances: raw zucchini, cucumbers, carrots or cauliflowerets; leftover cooked vegetables; canned peas, green beans or mixed vegetables.) Add salad greens and toss.

2 servings.

DATE-NUT BREAD

½ cup boiling water
½ cup raisins
½ cup cut-up dates
1 tablespoon plus 1½ teaspoons
   butter or margarine
¾ teaspoon soda
¾ cup plus 2 tablespoons
   all-purpose flour*
½ cup sugar
¼ teaspoon salt
1 egg
½ teaspoon vanilla
¼ cup chopped nuts

Heat oven to 350°. Grease and flour 1-pound coffee can. Pour boiling water on raisins, dates, butter and soda; let stand until cool. Beat in remaining ingredients. Pour into coffee can. Bake until wooden pick inserted in center comes out clean, 60 to 65 minutes. Remove from can; cool thoroughly before slicing.

*If using self-rising flour, decrease soda to ¼ teaspoon and omit salt.

BAKED APPLES

Heat oven to 350°. Core 2 baking apples (such as Rome Beauty, Golden Delicious or Greening). Remove 1-inch strip of skin around middle of each apple or pare upper half of each to prevent skin from splitting.

Place apples upright in small baking dish. Fill center of each apple with 1 to 2 tablespoons granulated or brown sugar, 1 teaspoon butter or margarine and ⅛ teaspoon cinnamon.

Pour water into baking dish to ¼-inch depth. Bake until apples are tender when pierced with fork, 30 to 40 minutes. (Time will vary with size and variety of apple.) If desired, spoon syrup in pan over apples several times during baking.

2 servings.

**Canadian-style Bacon
Oven-baked Beans
Mixed Vegetable Salad
Date-Nut Bread
Baked Apples**

Orange juice concentrate gives everyday pork chops a certain dash. For another kind of dash, consider cooking them in an electric skillet, right at the table.

ORANGE PORK CHOP SKILLET

4 pork loin or rib chops,
 ½ to ¾ inch thick
1 teaspoon salt
1 small onion, sliced
½ can (6-ounce size) frozen orange
 juice concentrate (thawed)*
2 tablespoons brown sugar
¼ teaspoon allspice
2 tablespoons lemon juice
2 tablespoons water
1 can (8 ounces) sweet potatoes
 in syrup, drained
1 small orange, sliced

In 10-inch skillet, brown chops over medium heat. Drain off fat. Sprinkle salt on chops. Arrange onion slices on chops. Mix orange juice concentrate, sugar, allspice, lemon juice and water; pour into skillet. Heat to boiling. Reduce heat; cover and simmer 30 minutes. Place sweet potatoes and orange slices on chops. Cover and cook until potatoes are hot, about 10 minutes.

2 servings.

*Leftover concentrate? Use in Orange Slush (page 22), as an ice-cream topping or for a speedy fruit drink.

TOSSED GREEN SALAD

3 to 4 cups bite-size pieces chilled
 crisp salad greens
¼ cup vegetables
 Oil-and-Vinegar Dressing (below)
 or favorite bottled dressing

Place greens and vegetables in bowl. Just before serving, pour dressing on ingredients and toss. Garnish salad as desired.

2 servings.

Oil-and-Vinegar Dressing

2 tablespoons salad oil
1 tablespoon wine, tarragon or
 cider vinegar or lemon juice
¼ teaspoon salt
½ small clove garlic, finely
 chopped, or dash garlic powder
 Dash freshly ground pepper

Shake all ingredients in tightly covered jar.

About ¼ cup.

Note: For perfect green salads, use chilled fresh salad greens. Vary the greens, vegetables and garnishes (see facing page). Tear greens into bite-size pieces; do not cut except when wedges, shredding or chunks are called for. Use just enough dressing to lightly coat the leaves.

QUICK DATE CAKE

1 package (14 ounces) date
 bar mix
½ cup hot water
2 eggs
1 teaspoon baking powder
½ cup chopped walnuts
 Confectioners' sugar

Heat oven to 375°. Grease baking pan, 8x8x2 inches. Mix date filling from date bar mix and hot water. Stir in crumbly mix, eggs, baking powder and nuts. Spread in pan. Bake until top springs back when touched lightly, about 30 minutes. Sprinkle confectioners' sugar on top.

Romaine, iceberg lettuce, tomato wedges, ripe olives, anchovies, crumbled blue or feta cheese

Leaf lettuce, escarole, avocado wedges, mushrooms, chopped peanuts, a sprinkle of curry powder

Iceberg lettuce, curly endive, tomato wedges, marinated artichoke hearts, zucchini, a sprinkle of grated Parmesan cheese

Leaf lettuce, radishes, cucumber, carrots, cauliflower (sliced on the diagonal), green onions

Iceberg chunks (line bowl with bright outer leaves), onion rings, ripe olives, corn chips, pickled red chili peppers

Spinach leaves, hardcooked egg, julienne strips of Swiss cheese, onion rings, bacon-flavored vegetable protein chips

Romaine, beets (or any leftover cooked vegetable), red onion rings, sour cream, black or red caviar

Boston or Bibb lettuce, drained canned mandarin orange segments, sliced water chestnuts

Spinach leaves, iceberg lettuce, cauliflowerets, pimiento-stuffed green olives, cherry tomatoes, green pepper rings

Something Special...

Tossed Salad Combos

SWEET-AND-SOUR RIBS

2 pounds pork spareribs or back
   ribs, cut into serving pieces
½ cup catsup
2 tablespoons brown sugar
¼ cup vinegar
2 tablespoons Worcestershire
   sauce
1 teaspoon celery seed
½ teaspoon chili powder
½ teaspoon salt
   Dash pepper
2 to 3 drops red pepper sauce

Place ribs meaty side up on rack in foil-lined shallow roasting pan. Mix remaining ingredients; pour about ⅓ cup sauce on ribs. Bake uncovered in 350° oven until done, 1½ to 2 hours, basting 3 or 4 times with remaining sauce.

For additional flavor and eye appeal, place 1 lemon, thinly sliced, on ribs during last hour of baking. If ribs are browning too quickly, cover loosely with aluminum foil.

2 servings.

Variation

Pineapple Ribs: Decrease vinegar to 2 tablespoons and add 1 can (8 ounces) crushed pineapple (with syrup) to the sauce ingredients.

BAKED ACORN SQUASH

Heat oven to 350°. Cut 1 acorn squash lengthwise in half. Place cut sides down in ungreased baking dish, 8x8x2 inches. Pour water into baking dish to ¼-inch depth. Bake uncovered 30 minutes. Turn squash cut sides up. Dot each half with butter or margarine; sprinkle with salt, pepper, and if desired, 1 tablespoon brown sugar or honey. Bake until squash is tender, 20 to 30 minutes.

2 servings.

CHINESE-STYLE CABBAGE

1 tablespoon salad oil
1½ cups finely shredded cabbage
½ cup thin diagonal slices
   celery
½ medium green pepper, cut into
   thin diagonal slices
⅓ cup chopped onion
½ teaspoon salt
   Dash pepper

Heat oil in 8-inch skillet; add vegetables and mix. Cover tightly and cook over medium-low heat, stirring occasionally, just until crisp-tender, 3 to 5 minutes. Sprinkle with salt and pepper. For extra flavor, add 1½ teaspoons soy sauce just before serving.

2 servings.

ROSY CINNAMON APPLES

Heat oven to 350°. Core 2 baking apples. Pare upper half of each apple to prevent skin from splitting. Or score skin in petal design. Place apples upright in small baking dish; fill center of each with 1 to 2 tablespoons brown sugar and 1 tablespoon red cinnamon candies. Pour water into baking dish to ¼-inch depth. Bake until apples are tender when pierced with fork, 30 to 40 minutes, spooning syrup on apples several times during baking. Serve warm, with cream or ice cream.

2 servings.

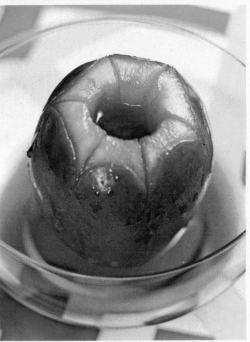

Confucius say: ''To remember dinner long time like elephant, wise person use trunk.'' Which is to say, an everyday meal can become a happening just by changing the scene—from dining table to coffee table or, as here, to the top of a handy trunk.

Discover what flavory herbs can do to make fish steaks special. And the asparagus "bundled" with pimiento adds a touch of unexpected elegance.

HERBED HALIBUT STEAKS

1 tablespoon butter or margarine
2 tablespoons lemon juice
1 package (12 ounces) frozen
    halibut steaks
1 teaspoon onion salt
¼ teaspoon lemon pepper
¼ to ½ teaspoon thyme, basil
    or marjoram
    Paprika
    Lemon wedges
    Parsley

Heat oven to 400°. In oven, melt butter in lemon juice in baking pan, 8x8x2 inches. Place frozen fish in pan; turn to coat other side with lemon butter. Sprinkle onion salt, lemon pepper and thyme on fish. Bake until fish flakes easily with fork, about 25 minutes. Sprinkle paprika on fish; serve with lemon wedges and parsley.

2 servings.

Variation

Herbed Salmon Steaks: Substitute 1 package (12 ounces) frozen salmon steaks for the halibut steaks.

BAKED POTATOES

Heat oven to 400°. Rub 2 medium baking potatoes with shortening if soft skins are desired. Prick with fork to allow steam to escape. Bake until tender, about 1 hour.

To serve, cut crisscross gash in each top; squeeze gently until some potato pops up through opening. Serve with butter or dairy sour cream.

2 servings.

SAVORY BEEF STEW

2 tablespoons shortening
½ to ¾ pound beef stew
    meat, cut into 1-inch
    pieces
1½ cups water
1 beef bouillon cube
½ clove garlic, finely chopped,
    or ⅛ teaspoon instant minced
    garlic
½ bay leaf, crumbled
1 teaspoon salt
⅛ teaspoon allspice
¼ teaspoon lemon juice
2 small onions or 1 medium
    onion, cut into quarters
2 medium potatoes, pared and
    cut into 1-inch cubes
2 medium carrots, cut into 1-inch
    pieces
½ package (10-ounce size) frozen
    green peas*
½ cup water
2 tablespoons flour

Melt shortening in 2-quart saucepan; brown meat. Add 1½ cups water, the bouillon cube, garlic, bay leaf, salt, allspice and lemon juice; heat to boiling, stirring occasionally. Reduce heat; cover and simmer until meat is almost tender, 1 to 1½ hours.

Add onions, potatoes and carrots; heat to boiling. Reduce heat; cover and simmer 20 minutes. Add peas; cook until vegetables are tender, about 10 minutes.

Shake ½ cup water and the flour in tightly covered jar until smooth. Stir into stew; heat to boiling, stirring constantly. Boil and stir 1 minute.

2 generous servings.

***Leftover frozen peas?** Cook as directed on package and serve as the vegetable in Orange Pork Chop Skillet menu (page 62) or use in Peas Almondine in Foil (page 58) or Paella (page 68).*

ORANGE AND GRAPEFRUIT SALAD

1 orange, pared and sectioned
1 grapefruit, pared and sectioned
    Crisp salad greens
    Ruby-red Dressing (below)

Arrange orange and grapefruit sections in pinwheel design on salad greens. Garnish with maraschino cherry if desired. Serve with Ruby-red Dressing.

2 servings.

Ruby-red Dressing
Beat ¼ cup currant or cranberry jelly and 2 tablespoons oil-and-vinegar dressing until smooth.

Time-saver: Substitute 1 can (11 ounces) mandarin orange segments, drained, for the orange and grapefruit.

CHOCOLATE CHIP COOKIES

⅓ cup shortening
⅓ cup butter or margarine, softened
½ cup granulated sugar
½ cup brown sugar (packed)
1 egg
1 teaspoon vanilla
1½ cups all-purpose flour*
½ teaspoon soda
½ teaspoon salt
½ cup chopped nuts
1 package (6 ounces) semisweet
    chocolate pieces

Heat oven to 375°. Mix thoroughly shortening, butter, sugars, egg and vanilla. Stir in remaining ingredients. (For a softer, rounder cookie, add ¼ cup flour.)

Drop dough by rounded teaspoonfuls 2 inches apart onto ungreased baking sheet. Bake until light brown, 8 to 10 minutes. Cool slightly before removing from baking sheet.

About 3½ dozen cookies.

*If using self-rising flour, omit soda and salt.

Savory Beef Stew
Orange and Grapefruit Salad
with Ruby-red Dressing
Celery Sticks
Rye Rolls
Chocolate Chip Cookies

Get away from it all—almost. Pretend you're in Valencia. Nibble on nuts and olives, sip fruit-and-wine Sangría, and the stage is set for this easy-do version of the classic Spanish paella.

PAELLA

2 tablespoons salad oil
1 to 1½ pounds chicken pieces
1 small onion, sliced
1 can (8 ounces) stewed tomatoes
1 teaspoon salt
1 teaspoon paprika
¼ teaspoon pepper
 Dash cayenne red pepper
½ package (6-ounce size) saffron rice (½ cup)
1½ cups chicken broth*
1 can (4½ ounces) medium shrimp, rinsed and drained
½ package (10-ounce size) frozen green peas, broken apart (about 1 cup)

Heat oil in Dutch oven; brown chicken. Remove chicken and set aside. Drain off fat.

Heat oven to 350°. Cook and stir onion, tomatoes and seasonings in Dutch oven until onion is tender, about 5 minutes. Stir in rice and broth; heat to boiling. Add chicken. Cover and bake 35 minutes. Add shrimp and peas; bake until chicken is tender, about 10 minutes. Serve in paella pan or shallow serving dish. Garnish with pimiento strips, parsley and artichoke hearts.

2 servings.

Note: Saffron rice hard to come by? You can substitute ½ cup uncooked regular rice plus a dash of saffron or ⅛ teaspoon turmeric.

*Chicken broth can be made by dissolving 1 chicken-bouillon cube in 1½ cups boiling water, or use canned chicken broth.

ORANGE-AVOCADO SALAD

1 orange, pared and sliced
1 avocado, pared and cut into wedges
1 small onion, sliced and separated into rings
 Crisp salad greens
 Orange Dressing (below)

Arrange orange slices, avocado wedges and onion rings on salad greens. Drizzle Orange Dressing on salads.

2 servings.

Orange Dressing

¼ cup salad oil
1 tablespoon lemon juice
½ teaspoon grated orange peel
2 tablespoons orange juice
1 tablespoon sugar
⅛ teaspoon salt
⅛ teaspoon dry mustard

Shake all ingredients in tightly covered jar.

½ cup.

Note: Use leftover dressing for Orange-Cucumber Salad (page 30).

Something to Know About...

At one time avocados seemed to be the private property of Californians—today we all get to share the wealth.

For best flavor, use only ripe avocados. (A ripe avocado will yield to gentle pressure when held between the palms of your hands.) If necessary, leave at room temperature for several days to ripen.

To use, cut the avocado lengthwise into halves. (Your knife will hit the large hard seed.) Twist gently to separate. To remove the seed easily, strike it with a sharp knife, twist the seed gently and lift it out. With a paring knife, carefully strip off the avocado skin. If the avocado will not be used immediately, drizzle the cut surfaces with lemon juice to prevent discoloration.

TUNA SALAD IN TOMATO CUPS

1 can (6½ ounces) tuna, drained
  and separated into chunks
¼ cup chopped celery
2 tablespoons chopped green pepper
1 tablespoon finely chopped onion
½ teaspoon lemon juice
½ teaspoon soy sauce
  Dash white pepper
¼ cup mayonnaise or salad dressing
2 medium tomatoes
  Salt
⅓ cup chow mein noodles or
  shoestring potatoes
  Celery leaves
  Crisp salad greens

Tuna Salad in Tomato Cups
Fresh Vegetable Relishes
(page 46)
Popovers
Orange-Pineapple
Ice Cream

Toss tuna, celery, green pepper, onion, lemon juice, soy sauce, pepper and mayonnaise in bowl. Cover and chill.

Remove stem ends of tomatoes. Place tomatoes cut sides down; cut each into sixths, cutting to within 1 inch of bottom. Spread sections apart to form cups. Sprinkle salt on sections.

Fold noodles into tuna mixture. Spoon salad into tomato cups. Garnish cups with celery leaves and place on salad greens.

2 servings.

Variations

Ham Salad in Pineapple Boats: Substitute 1 cup cubed cooked ham for the tuna; omit tomatoes and salad greens and serve salad in Pineapple Boats: Cut fresh pineapple lengthwise in half through green top. Cut along curved edges with grapefruit knife; remove fruit and toss with salad. Invert shells to drain.

Crabmeat Salad in Avocado Halves: Substitute 1 can (7½ ounces) crabmeat, drained and cartilage removed, for the tuna; omit tomatoes and salad greens and serve salad in Avocado Halves: Cut unpeeled avocado lengthwise in half; remove pit. Brush halves with lemon juice; sprinkle with salt.

POPOVERS

1 egg
½ cup milk
½ cup quick-mixing flour*
¼ teaspoon salt

Heat oven to 450°. Grease generously 3 deep custard cups (6-ounce size) or 4 medium muffin cups. Beat egg slightly with fork; add milk, flour and salt and stir with fork just until smooth. Do not overbeat.

Fill custard cups ½ full, muffin cups ¾ full. Bake 20 minutes. Lower oven temperature to 350° and bake until deep golden brown, about 20 minutes longer. Immediately remove popovers from cups; serve hot with butter.

3 or 4 popovers.

*If using regular all-purpose flour, beat ingredients with rotary beater.

Note: This recipe can be doubled to make 6 to 8 popovers. Leftover popovers can be reheated on ungreased baking sheet in 350° oven about 5 minutes. Or wrap in aluminum foil and freeze. Remove foil and heat about 10 minutes.

ORANGE-PINEAPPLE ICE CREAM

Soften 1 pint vanilla ice cream slightly. Stir in ½ can (6-ounce size) frozen orange-pineapple juice concentrate (thawed). Spoon ice cream into original container or refrigerator tray and freeze until firm.

2 servings.

Variations

Cinnamon Ice Cream: Substitute 1 teaspoon cinnamon for the concentrate.

Coffee Ice Cream: Substitute 1 to 2 teaspoons powdered instant coffee for the concentrate.

Nesselrode Ice Cream: Substitute 2 tablespoons Nesselrode for the concentrate.

Pork and apples—always a favorite twosome. Here they're baked side by side, as flavory main dish and crunch-topped dessert. Buttery corn on the cob (fresh or frozen) provides the perfect all-American accent. Reminder: Fresh corn is best when eaten as soon after picking as possible. Look for green husks and fresh silk. Refrigerate until ready to use, then husk and remove silk *just* before cooking.

LEMON BARBECUED PORK CHOPS

2 pork loin or rib chops, ¾ to
   1 inch thick
½ teaspoon salt
2 thin slices onion
2 thin slices lemon
2 tablespoons brown sugar
2 tablespoons catsup

Heat oven to 350°. Trim excess fat from chops. Place chops in ungreased baking pan, 8x8x2 inches; season with salt. Top each chop with 1 slice onion, 1 slice lemon, 1 tablespoon sugar and 1 tablespoon catsup. Cover tightly with aluminum foil and bake 30 minutes. Uncover; baste chops and bake until done, about 30 minutes.

2 servings.

CORN ON THE COB

In large saucepan, heat enough water to boiling to cover 2 to 4 ears corn. Do not add salt—salt toughens corn. If desired, add 1 teaspoon sugar and 1 teaspoon lemon juice for each 2 quarts water. Drop corn carefully into boiling water. Cover and cook 5 to 8 minutes, depending on size of corn. Drain. Serve with butter, salt and pepper. For variety, try one of these other favorite seasonings mixed with soft butter: basil, cayenne red pepper, celery seed, chili powder or rosemary leaves.

2 servings.

LETTUCE WEDGES WITH ROQUEFORT DRESSING

½ cup dairy sour cream
¼ cup crumbled Roquefort or
   blue cheese (about 1 ounce)
½ teaspoon lemon juice
¼ teaspoon salt
2 lettuce wedges

Mix all ingredients except lettuce wedges. Cover and refrigerate at least 1 hour to blend flavors. Add small amount milk or light cream if necessary for proper consistency. Spoon onto lettuce wedges.

2 servings.

APPLE CRISP

2 cups sliced pared tart
   apples (2 medium)
1 tablespoon water
½ teaspoon lemon juice
½ teaspoon cinnamon
¼ cup granulated sugar or brown
   sugar (packed)
3 tablespoons flour
2 tablespoons butter or margarine

Heat oven to 350°. Place apple slices in ungreased 1¾-cup casserole. Sprinkle water, lemon juice and cinnamon on apples. Mix remaining ingredients until crumbly; sprinkle on apples. Bake uncovered until apples are tender and topping is golden brown, about 30 minutes. Serve warm. Top with light cream or ice cream if you like.

2 servings.

**Lemon Barbecued Pork
Chops**
Corn on the Cob
**Lettuce Wedges with
Roquefort Dressing**
Hot Rolls
Apple Crisp

SALMON LOAF

1 can (8 ounces) salmon, drained (reserve liquid)
Milk plus reserved salmon liquid to measure ⅓ cup
1 egg, slightly beaten
¾ cup cracker crumbs
1 tablespoon lemon juice
1 tablespoon chopped onion
Dash pepper
Egg Sauce (below)

Heat oven to 350°. Flake salmon, removing skin and bone. Mix in remaining ingredients except sauce. In buttered baking pan, 8x8x2 inches, shape mixture into a loaf. Bake uncovered until center is firm, about 30 minutes. Serve with Egg Sauce.

2 servings.

Egg Sauce

1 tablespoon butter or margarine
1 tablespoon flour
¼ teaspoon salt
⅛ teaspoon pepper
¾ cup milk
1 hard-cooked egg, diced

Melt butter in small saucepan. Mix in flour, salt and pepper. Cook over low heat, stirring until mixture is smooth and bubbly. Remove from heat and stir in milk. Heat to boiling, stirring constantly. Boil and stir 1 minute. Stir in egg.

¾ cup.

Variations

Cucumber Sauce: Omit egg and stir in ¼ cup shredded or thinly sliced cucumber and dash cayenne red pepper.

Dill Sauce: Omit egg and stir in ½ teaspoon dill weed and dash nutmeg.

LEMON-BUTTERED BROCCOLI

Heat oven to 350°. In ungreased 1-quart casserole, place 1 package (10 ounces) frozen broccoli spears, 1 tablespoon butter or margarine and 2 teaspoons lemon juice. Cover and bake until tender, about 35 minutes.

2 servings.

FRESH FRUIT SALAD

1 grapefruit, pared and sectioned
¼ cantaloupe, pared and cut into pieces
1 cup fresh strawberries, halved
Lime-Honey Dressing (page 60)
Lettuce

Toss fruit and dressing. Serve salad on lettuce.

2 servings.

HOT FUDGE PUDDING CAKE

⅓ cup all-purpose flour*
¼ cup granulated sugar
1 tablespoon cocoa
¾ teaspoon baking powder
⅛ teaspoon salt
3 tablespoons milk
1 tablespoon salad oil
⅓ cup chopped nuts
⅓ cup brown sugar (packed)
1 tablespoon cocoa
⅔ cup hot water

Heat oven to 350°. Mix all ingredients except brown sugar, 1 tablespoon cocoa and the hot water. Pour into ungreased 1-quart casserole. Mix brown sugar and 1 tablespoon cocoa; sprinkle on batter. Pour hot water on batter. Bake 30 to 35 minutes. Serve warm. Top with whipped cream or ice cream if you wish.

2 servings.

*If using self-rising flour, omit baking powder and salt.

Lamb chops don't have to deal your budget a body blow. Not if you look for cuts from the shoulder. And taste what a hint of mint (traditional with lamb) can do to rouse carrots out of the ho-hum category. Another time use mint to perk up peas.

LAMB CHOPS HAWAIIAN

    2 lamb shoulder chops (arm or
         blade), ½ inch thick
    1 can (8¼ ounces) pineapple chunks,
         drained (reserve syrup)
    2 tablespoons soy sauce
    2 tablespoons vinegar
    ¼ teaspoon dry mustard
    1 tablespoon salad oil
    2 tablespoons brown sugar
    ¾ teaspoon cornstarch
    1½ cups hot cooked rice
         Parsley

Place meat in shallow glass dish. Mix reserved pineapple syrup, the soy sauce, vinegar and mustard; pour on meat. Cover and refrigerate at least 4 hours, turning meat occasionally.

Remove meat from marinade; reserve marinade. Heat oil in 8-inch skillet; brown meat over medium heat. Pour ¼ cup reserved marinade on chops. Cover and simmer until tender, 30 to 40 minutes.

Mix sugar and cornstarch in small saucepan. Stir in remaining reserved marinade. Heat to boiling, stirring constantly. Reduce heat; simmer 2 to 3 minutes. Stir in pineapple; heat through, about 1 minute. Serve chops with pineapple sauce and rice. Garnish with parsley.

2 servings.

MINTED CARROTS

4 or 5 medium carrots
1 tablespoon mint-flavored jelly
    or 1 teaspoon finely snipped
    mint leaves

Cut carrots lengthwise into ⅜-inch-wide strips. Heat 1 inch salted water (½ teaspoon salt to 1 cup water) to boiling. Add carrots. Cover and heat to boiling; cook until tender, about 10 minutes. Drain. Dot hot carrots with jelly; stir lightly to glaze carrots.

2 servings.

VELVET CRUMB CAKE WITH BROILED TOPPING

Bake Velvet Crumb Cake as directed on package of buttermilk baking mix, Spread Broiled Topping (below) on ⅓ of warm cake. Cover remaining cake with aluminum foil. Broil cake with top 3 inches from heat until topping is golden, about 3 minutes.

2 servings.

Broiled Topping

    2 tablespoons brown sugar
    2 tablespoons soft butter or
         margarine
    1 tablespoon half-and-half
    ¼ cup coconut
    2 tablespoons chopped nuts

Mix all ingredients.

Note: Wrap remaining cake in aluminum foil (2 servings in each package) and store in refrigerator or freezer. To serve warm, heat in foil in 400° oven 10 minutes (if frozen, heat 30 to 35 minutes). Top with apricot or peach jam, cranberry relish, blueberry or cherry pie filling, fresh or frozen (thawed) strawberries, Pineapple Sauce (page 34) or vanilla ice cream and chocolate sauce.

**Lamb Chops Hawaiian
Fluffy White Rice
Minted Carrots
Tossed Spinach Salad
(page 29)
Velvet Crumb Cake with
Broiled Topping**

DELUXE BAKED CHICKEN

  2 tablespoons salad oil
  ¼ cup all-purpose flour
  ½ teaspoon salt
  ¼ teaspoon paprika
  ⅛ teaspoon pepper
1½ pounds chicken pieces
  ¼ cup chicken broth
  2 tablespoons sherry or apple juice
  1 small clove garlic, crushed

Heat oil in large skillet. Measure flour, salt, paprika and pepper into plastic or paper bag. Shake chicken, 2 or 3 pieces at a time, in bag until thoroughly coated. Brown chicken in oil over medium heat.

Heat oven to 350°. Place chicken skin side up in ungreased baking pan, 9x9x2 inches. Mix broth, sherry and garlic. Pour ⅓ of broth mixture on chicken. Cover with aluminum foil and bake until tender, 45 to 50 minutes, basting occasionally with remaining broth mixture. Uncover last 5 minutes of baking time to crisp chicken.

2 servings.

CHILI PEPPER CASSEROLE

½ can (4-ounce size) peeled green
   chili peppers*
1 cup shredded process Cheddar
   cheese (about 4 ounces)
1 egg
½ cup milk
¼ cup buttermilk baking mix

Heat oven to 350°. Grease 2- to 2½-cup casserole. Rinse peppers to remove seeds. Place peppers in single layer in casserole. Sprinkle cheese on peppers. Beat egg thoroughly; beat in milk and baking mix and pour onto cheese. Bake until golden brown and puffy, about 30 minutes.

2 servings.

***Leftover chili peppers?** Chop and use as a spicy substitution for pimiento.

FRESH VEGETABLES VINAIGRETTE

1 small zucchini or cucumber,
   thinly sliced
1 carrot, cut crosswise into
   ¼-inch slices
¼ cup cauliflowerets
¼ cup oil-and-vinegar dressing
2 lettuce cups

Toss all ingredients except lettuce cups in bowl. Chill at least 2 hours, tossing occasionally. Serve in lettuce cups.

2 servings.

LEMON SHERBET WITH RASPBERRY-CURRANT SAUCE

  1 package (10 ounces) frozen
    raspberries, thawed
  ½ cup currant jelly
1½ teaspoons cornstarch
  1 tablespoon cold water
  ½ pint lemon sherbet

Heat raspberries (with syrup) and currant jelly to boiling, stirring frequently. Mix cornstarch and water until smooth. Stir into raspberry-currant mixture. Cook, stirring constantly, until mixture thickens and boils. Boil and stir 1 minute. Cool, and if desired, strain.

Scoop sherbet into dessert dishes. Pour sauce on top.

2 servings.

Note: Leftover sauce can be stored in refrigerator and served later in the week on ice cream or custard.

Planning Ahead

Dinners that star a "big" meat buy—with repeat performances as sparkling as First Night

Corned beef for two? Sure . . . when you start with a small one and are enterprising with the extras. But for starters, this traditional menu is unbeatable. Especially with the Little Loaves and choice of desserts.

Corned Beef and Cabbage with Horseradish Sauce
Anadama Batter Bread
Creamy Peach Pudding or Quick Mocha Dessert
Ginger Cookies

CORNED BEEF AND CABBAGE

2- to 3-pound beef corned brisket
2 small onions
4 small carrots
2 small potatoes, pared and halved
½ green cabbage, cut into wedges
Horseradish Sauce (right)

Cook meat as directed on package. If directions are not available, place meat in Dutch oven; cover with hot water. Heat to boiling. Reduce heat; cover tightly and simmer until tender, 3 to 3½ hours.

About 20 minutes before meat is tender, skim fat from liquid, then add onions, carrots and potatoes. Cover and simmer 20 minutes. Remove meat and keep warm.

Add cabbage to liquid; simmer uncovered until vegetables are tender, 10 to 15 minutes. To carve meat, cut thin diagonal slices across the grain. Serve with Horseradish Sauce.

2 servings.

Horseradish Sauce

⅓ cup mayonnaise or dairy sour cream
1 tablespoon horseradish
Dash paprika
Dash dry mustard

Mix all ingredients. Refrigerate until serving time.

About ⅓ cup.

ANADAMA BATTER BREAD

¾ cup boiling water
½ cup yellow cornmeal
3 tablespoons shortening
¼ cup molasses
2 teaspoons salt
1 package active dry yeast
¼ cup warm water (105 to 115°)
1 egg
2¾ cups all-purpose flour*

Grease loaf pan, 8½x4½x2¾ or 9x5x3 inches. In large mixer bowl, mix boiling water, the cornmeal, shortening, molasses and salt; cool to lukewarm.

Dissolve yeast in warm water. Add yeast, egg and half the flour to cornmeal mixture. Beat on medium speed 2 minutes, scraping bowl frequently, or beat 300 vigorous strokes by hand. Stir in remaining flour until smooth. Spread evenly in pan. Batter will be sticky; smooth top of loaf with floured hand.

Let rise in warm place until batter reaches top of 8½-inch pan or 1 inch from top of 9-inch pan, about 1½ hours. Sprinkle small amount of cornmeal and salt on loaf.

Heat oven to 375°. Bake until loaf sounds hollow when tapped, 50 to 55 minutes. Remove loaf from pan; place on wire rack. Brush top with melted butter or shortening. Cool before cutting.

1 loaf.

*If using self-rising flour, omit salt.

Variations

Little Loaves: Grease 6 miniature loaf pans, 4½x2½x1½ inches. Divide batter among pans and let rise until it just reaches the tops of pans, about 1½ hours. Bake 30 to 35 minutes.

Oatmeal Batter Bread: Substitute ½ cup oats for the yellow cornmeal.

CREAMY PEACH PUDDING

½ can (17.5-ounce size) vanilla
  pudding (1 cup)
¼ cup dairy sour cream
1 can (8 ounces) sliced peaches,
  drained

Mix pudding and sour cream. Layer pudding and peaches in each dessert dish.

2 servings.

QUICK MOCHA DESSERT

Blend ½ can (17.5-ounce size) chocolate pudding (1 cup) and 1½ teaspoons powdered instant coffee. Divide between dessert dishes and garnish with whipped topping and mint leaves.

2 servings.

GINGER COOKIES

Heat oven to 375°. Mix 1 package (14.5 ounces) gingerbread mix and ½ cup water. Drop dough by teaspoonfuls about 2 inches apart onto lightly greased baking sheet. Bake until almost no imprint remains when touched, 10 to 12 minutes.

About 3 dozen cookies.

Variation

Mincemeat Ginger Drops: Stir in 1 cup prepared mincemeat and ½ cup chopped nuts.

"Corned Beef Revisited": a clever variety show featuring robust Reuben sandwiches, a savory skillet hash, a reprise of corned beef and cabbage (only easier), a cheesy casserole (easier still).

CORNED BEEF SKILLET HASH

1 cup chopped cooked corned beef
1 cup chopped cooked potatoes
¼ cup finely chopped onion
1 tablespoon snipped parsley
¼ teaspoon salt
⅛ teaspoon pepper
3 tablespoons salad oil
½ cup tomato juice

Mix meat, potatoes, onion, parsley, salt and pepper. Heat oil in 8-inch skillet. Spread meat mixture evenly in skillet; brown over medium heat, turning frequently with wide spatula, about 10 minutes. Stir in tomato juice. Reduce heat; cover and cook until liquid is absorbed, about 10 minutes.

2 servings.

QUICK CORNED BEEF AND CABBAGE

2 tablespoons butter or margarine
1½ cups coarsely shredded cabbage
½ package (6-ounce size) hash brown potatoes with onions (about 1¼ cups)
¾ cup water
½ teaspoon salt
1 cup cut-up cooked corned beef

Melt butter in 8-inch skillet. Stir in cabbage, potatoes, water and salt. Cook over medium-high heat until liquid is absorbed and bottom is brown, 8 to 12 minutes. Sprinkle meat into skillet; turn mixture with wide spatula and cook until meat is hot, about 3 minutes.

2 servings.

REUBEN GRILL

2 tablespoons Thousand Island dressing
4 slices rye or pumpernickel bread
2 slices Swiss cheese
½ cup sauerkraut, drained
½ pound thinly sliced cooked corned beef
Soft butter or margarine

Spread dressing on 2 slices bread. Top with cheese, sauerkraut, meat and remaining bread slices. Spread butter on outsides of sandwiches. Grill in skillet over low to medium heat until brown and cheese is melted, 5 to 7 minutes on each side.

2 servings.

CORNED BEEF AND MACARONI CASSEROLE

Heat oven to 375° Measure contents of 1 package (7.25 ounces) macaroni and cheese; divide in half (approximately ¾ cup macaroni and 2 tablespoons Sauce Mix).*

In ungreased 1-quart casserole, mix half the macaroni, 2 tablespoons Sauce Mix, 1½ teaspoons butter or margarine and 1¼ cups boiling water. Stir in 1 cup cut-up cooked corned beef. Cover and bake 20 to 25 minutes. Stir before serving.

2 servings.

*To store remaining mix, close package securely and use within 2 weeks. Delicious with hamburgers, frankfurters, chicken or luncheon meat.

Variations

Tuna and Macaroni Casserole: Omit corned beef and stir in 1 can (6½ ounces) tuna, drained and flaked.

Chicken and Macaroni Casserole: Omit corned beef and stir in 1 can (5 ounces) boned chicken, cut up, and 2 tablespoons sliced pimiento-stuffed olives.

Carving can be as easy as 1,2,3: 1—a good, sharp carving knife; 2—properly cooked meat; 3—a little practice.

Take good care of your knife—it's your most important tool. Store it sheathed or boxed to protect the edge, wash it (separately) after every use and always carve on a cutting board.

Be sure to let a roast "set" before carving (see specific recipes). This allows the meat to become a little firmer and therefore easier to cut.

Just before the "setting" time is up, remember to remove all strings and skewers from the roast—though it's a good idea to leave one or two strings on a rolled roast so that it won't fall apart when you carve it.

Check which way the grain of the meat runs, then slice at right angles to the grain. This way the muscle fibers of each slice will be short—and the shorter the fibers, the more tender the meat. Flank steak, beef corned brisket and other cuts that are too thin to cut at right angles should be sliced at a slant across the grain. Whatever kind of meat you choose, try to carve slices that are uniform in size and thickness.

Something Special...

Carving Cues

Rolled Roast

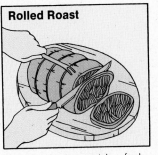

Secure roast with fork. Slice downward across grain of meat with straight, even strokes, making each slice about ¼ inch thick.

Flank Steak

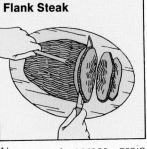

Always cut across grain of meat at a slanted angle into thin, even slices, keeping slices uniform in thickness.

Porterhouse Steak

Cut around bone; remove. Carve 1-inch slices across width of steak. (Each serving should have a portion of the tenderloin.)

Pork Loin Roast

Have retailer saw backbone free from ribs for easy carving; after cooking, remove bone. Cut slices on each side of rib bones.

Leg of Lamb

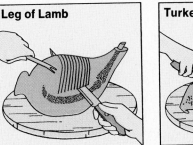

Cut 2 or 3 slices from thin side; turn onto cut side. Make vertical slices to bone; cut horizontally along bone to free slices.

Turkey

Remove leg. Make deep horizontal cut into breast above wing. Starting halfway up, carve thin slices to the cut, working upward.

Something Special...

Yeast Rolls

In medium mixing bowl, dissolve **1 package active dry yeast** in **1 cup warm water** (110 to 115°). Stir in **¼ cup sugar, 1 teaspoon salt, 1 egg, ¼ cup shortening** and **1½ cups all-purpose flour** (if using self-rising flour, omit salt). Beat vigorously with wooden spoon until batter falls from spoon in "sheets." Using first the spoon and then your hands, mix in up to **2¼ cups additional flour**—use just enough so that dough leaves side of bowl almost clean. Since flour absorbs moisture or dries out, depending on the humidity, use only as much as needed. Dough will be rough, lumpy and sticky at this stage. Turn dough onto lightly floured board. Knead until dough is smooth and elastic, about 5 minutes.

Place in greased bowl; turn dough to grease all sides. Cover; let rise in warm place (85°) until double, about 1½ hours.

Punch down dough. Shape rolls (right). Let rise 20 minutes.

Heat oven to 400°. Bake rolls until golden brown, 15 to 20 minutes.

24 Cloverleafs or 32 Crescents.

Note: To freeze rolls, wrap in heavy-duty aluminum foil (4 in each package), label and freeze. Heat foil-wrapped rolls on rack in 350° oven 20 minutes.

Beat until batter "sheets" from spoon, then add just enough of remaining flour so that dough leaves side of bowl almost clean.

To knead, fold dough toward you and push away with heels of hands in rocking motion; rotate ¼ turn. Repeat until smooth.

To test if dough has doubled in bulk, press 2 fingers into dough; impression will remain if it has risen enough.

CLOVERLEAFS: Shape the dough into 1-inch balls. Place 3 balls in each greased muffin cup. Brush rolls with soft butter.

CRESCENTS: Divide dough in half. Roll each half into 12-inch circle. Brush with soft butter. Cut into 16 wedges and roll up.

Place rolls with points underneath on greased baking sheet; curve ends slightly. Brush rolls with soft butter.

What a feast—a real old-time baked ham dinner. And no, you don't have to keep on eating it day after day. Just cut in portions called for by the recipes on page 99, wrap for freezing (be sure to label) and use within 3 to 4 weeks.

Idea: A tiny canned ham can be a life-saver-for-two (especially the 1½-pound size). Try to keep one on your "emergency" shelf. But watch it—some need refrigeration, some don't. Look to the label.

BAKED HAM

Place ham fat side up on rack in shallow roasting pan. Insert meat thermometer so tip is in center of thickest part of meat and does not touch bone or rest in fat.

Roast uncovered in 325° oven until done (see Timetable), using thermometer reading as final guide. Ham is easier to carve if allowed to "set" 15 to 20 minutes after removing from oven. Since meat continues to cook after removal from oven, if ham is to set, it should be removed when thermometer registers 5° lower than desired doneness.

	TIMETABLE	
Cut	Approximate Cooking Time (Minutes per Lb.)	Meat Thermometer Reading
Ham (fully cooked)		
Half 5 to 7 lbs.	18 to 24	140°
Shank or rump (butt) portion 3 to 4 lbs.	18 to 24	140°
Ham (cook before eating)		
Half 5 to 7 lbs.	22 to 25	160°
Shank or rump (butt) portion 3 to 4 lbs.	35 to 40	160°
Smoked Shoulder Roll 2 to 4 lbs.	35 to 40	170°

PECAN SWEET POTATOES

Heat oven to 325°. Place 1 can (8 ounces) sweet potatoes in syrup, drained, in ungreased 1¾-cup casserole. Sprinkle with 3 tablespoons brown sugar and dot with 1 tablespoon butter. Bake uncovered until hot and bubbly, 25 to 30 minutes. Sprinkle with 1 to 2 tablespoons broken pecans.

2 servings.

CAULIFLOWER WITH NUTMEG BUTTER

Heat 1 inch salted water (½ teaspoon salt to 1 cup water) to boiling. Add 1 small cauliflower. Cover; heat to boiling. Cook until tender, 12 to 15 minutes. Drain; turn into serving dish. Dot with butter and sprinkle with nutmeg.

2 servings.

MOLDED LIME-PINEAPPLE SALAD

1 cup boiling water
1 package (3 ounces) lime-flavored gelatin
1 can (8¾ ounces) crushed pineapple, drained (reserve syrup)
Lettuce
Mayonnaise

Pour boiling water on gelatin in bowl; stir until gelatin is dissolved. Add enough water to reserved pineapple syrup to measure 1 cup; stir into gelatin. Chill until thickened but not set.

Stir in pineapple. Pour into 4 to 6 individual molds or one 4-cup mold. Chill until firm. Place 2 servings on lettuce and top each with mayonnaise. Serve remaining gelatin topped with whipped cream as a dessert the next day.

2 servings—and 2 to 4 for another day.

Baked Ham
Pecan Sweet Potatoes
Cauliflower with Nutmeg Butter
Molded Lime-Pineapple Salad
Brown and Serve Rolls
Mocha Parfaits (page 26)

Four impressive planned-overs from That Ham. Note especially the unique Ham 'n Cheese Supper Bread. Be sure to serve it warm, with soup and a jumbo salad.

EGGS BENEDICT

2 eggs
1 envelope (1¼ ounces) hollandaise
    sauce mix
2 thin slices cooked ham
1 English muffin, split and toasted

Heat water (1½ to 2 inches) in saucepan or skillet to boiling; reduce heat to simmer. Break eggs, 1 at a time, into custard cup or saucer; holding cup or saucer close to surface of water, slip egg into water. Cook until eggs reach desired doneness, 3 to 5 minutes.

While eggs cook, prepare hollandaise sauce as directed on package. Place slice of ham on each muffin half, then top with an egg and half the hollandaise sauce.

2 servings.

CHILI-BEAN SKILLET

1 cup cubed cooked ham
½ cup sliced celery
¼ cup chopped onion
¼ cup chopped green pepper
    Dash instant minced garlic
½ teaspoon salt
2 tablespoons salad oil
1 can (8 ounces) pork and beans
1 can (8 ounces) lima beans
⅓ cup chili sauce

In 8-inch skillet, cook and stir ham, celery, onion, green pepper, garlic and salt in oil until onion is tender. Drain off fat. Stir in pork and beans, lima beans (with liquid) and chili sauce; simmer uncovered until hot, about 10 minutes.

2 servings.

Pictured at left: Scalloped Potatoes with Ham, Ham 'n Cheese Supper Bread and Chili-Bean Skillet

HAM 'N CHEESE SUPPER BREAD

1 cup buttermilk baking mix
½ cup chopped cooked ham
2 tablespoons instant minced onion
1 egg
⅓ cup milk
1 tablespoon salad oil
¼ teaspoon prepared mustard
1 cup shredded Cheddar cheese
    (about 4 ounces)
1 tablespoon sesame seed

Heat oven to 350°. Grease 1-quart casserole. Mix baking mix, ham, onion, egg, milk, oil, mustard and ⅔ cup of the cheese. Spread in casserole. Sprinkle remaining cheese and the sesame seed on top. Bake until top is golden brown, 30 to 35 minutes. Serve warm.

2 servings.

Note: Wrap leftover bread in aluminum foil and refrigerate or freeze. Heat in wrapping in 400° oven until warm, about 10 minutes (if frozen, 30 to 35 minutes).

SCALLOPED POTATOES WITH HAM

Heat oven to 400°. Measure contents of 1 package (5.5 ounces) scalloped potatoes; divide in half (approximately 1 cup potato slices and 3 tablespoons sauce mix).* Place potato slices in ungreased 1-quart casserole; sprinkle half the sauce mix on potato slices. Add 1 cup cut-up cooked ham and stir in half the amounts of water and milk called for on package. Bake uncovered until potatoes are tender and golden brown, 25 to 30 minutes.

2 servings.

*To store remaining mix, close package securely and use within 2 weeks. Make Quick Scalloped Potatoes (page 40) and serve with pork chops, ham, frankfurters or hamburgers.

A lordly beef roast. Who can resist it? Figure on about ½ pound per serving—less for boneless, a little more for bone-in. If leftovers are minimal, you can refrigerate promptly and use within one or two days. (See page 115 for a refresher on freezing.) Choose the rolled rump if you're watching the budget. Another time try the boneless rib for a fabulous feast for two.

Roast Beef with Oven-browned Potatoes

Sautéed Cherry Tomatoes

Marinated Asparagus Spears

Lemon Sherbet with Raspberry-Currant Sauce (page 74)

ROAST BEEF WITH OVEN-BROWNED POTATOES

Place roast fat side up on rack in shallow roasting pan. Season with salt and pepper before, during or after roasting (salt goes into roast only ¼ to ½ inch). Insert meat thermometer so tip is in center of thickest part of meat and does not rest in fat.

Roast uncovered in 325° oven until done (see Timetable), using thermometer reading as final guide. About 1½ hours before roast is done, pare 2 medium baking potatoes. If you wish, make thin crosswise cuts almost through potatoes. Heat 1 inch salted water (½ teaspoon salt to 1 cup water) to boiling. Add potatoes. Cover and heat to boiling; cook 10 minutes. Drain.

Place potatoes in meat drippings in roasting pan; turn each potato to coat with fat. Or brush potatoes with melted butter or margarine and place on rack with meat. Turning potatoes once, bake until tender and golden brown, 1¼ to 1½ hours. Season with salt and pepper.

Roasts are easier to carve if allowed to "set" 15 to 20 minutes after removing from oven. Since meat continues to cook after removal from oven, if roast is to set, it should be removed from oven when thermometer registers 5° lower than the desired doneness. Serve with meat juices or Pan Gravy (page 37).

2 servings.

TIMETABLE		
Cut	Approximate Cooking Time (Minutes per Lb.)	Meat Thermometer Reading
Boneless Rib	32	140° (rare)
5 to 7 lbs.	38	160° (medium)
	48	170° (well)
Rib Eye	18 to 20	140° (rare)
(Delmonico)*	20 to 22	160° (medium)
4 to 5 lbs.	22 to 24	170° (well)
Tip Roast	35 to 40	150 to 170°
(high quality)		
3½ to 4 lbs.		
Rolled Rump	25 to 30	150 to 170°
(high quality)		
4 to 5 lbs.		

*Roast at 350°.

SAUTÉED CHERRY TOMATOES

Remove stem ends from ½ pint cherry tomatoes. Prick each tomato several times. Melt 1 tablespoon butter or margarine in 8-inch skillet. Cook and stir tomatoes in butter over medium heat until heated through, about 3 minutes. For a garnish, sprinkle snipped chives on top.

2 servings.

MARINATED ASPARAGUS SPEARS

1 package (10 ounces) frozen asparagus spears
½ cup Italian dressing
Lettuce leaves
Pimiento strips

Cook asparagus spears as directed on package. Drain and turn into bowl. Pour dressing on hot asparagus; cover and refrigerate 2 to 3 hours. Serve spears on lettuce leaves and garnish with pimiento strips.

2 servings.

Now revel in your beef leftovers! Savor Beef Rolls in Wine, a recipe you may well want to double to share with a pair of discriminating friends. Enjoy a superb main-dish salad. And by all means, get familiar with the quick skillet dish—it lets you shine even when you've plain run out of time! (We've pictured all of them on page 75.)

BEEF ROLLS IN WINE

1 can (2 ounces) mushroom stems
    and pieces, drained and chopped
2 tablespoons chopped onion
4 thin slices cooked roast beef
1 tablespoon salad oil
1 can (16 ounces) whole carrots,
    drained (reserve liquid)
3 tablespoons red wine
3 tablespoons gravy mix (dry)
¼ teaspoon salt
¼ teaspoon pepper
    Dash thyme
    Snipped parsley

Mix mushrooms and onion; place ¼ of mixture on center of each beef slice. Roll up and fasten with wooden picks. Heat oil in 8-inch skillet; brown rolls. Add enough water to reserved carrot liquid to measure 1 cup. Stir carrot liquid, wine, gravy mix, salt, pepper and thyme into skillet. Heat to boiling. Reduce heat; cover and simmer 10 minutes. Add carrots; simmer until hot, about 10 minutes. Garnish with parsley.

2 servings.

CHILI CHEF'S SALAD

½ cup julienne strips cooked meat
    (beef, ham, tongue, luncheon meat)
½ cup julienne strips cooked
    chicken or turkey
½ cup julienne strips Swiss cheese
¼ cup chopped green onion
¼ cup sliced celery
8 cups bite-size pieces lettuce
    (iceberg and/or romaine)
⅓ cup mayonnaise or salad dressing
⅓ cup chili sauce
    Ripe olives
1 hard-cooked egg, cut into wedges

Reserve few strips of meat, chicken and cheese for garnish. In large bowl, toss remaining meat, chicken, cheese, the onion, celery and lettuce. Mix mayonnaise and chili sauce; pour on salad and toss. Garnish with reserved meat, chicken and cheese, the olives and egg wedges.

2 generous servings.

HERBED BEEF AND ONIONS

2 tablespoons butter or margarine
1 medium onion, sliced and
    separated into rings
4 slices cooked roast beef
2 teaspoons vinegar
1 tablespoon butter or margarine,
    softened
⅛ teaspoon thyme, tarragon or
    marjoram leaves

Melt 2 tablespoons butter in 8-inch skillet; cook and stir onion until tender, about 5 minutes. Remove onion from skillet and keep warm.

Add meat to skillet; brown quickly on both sides and sprinkle with vinegar. Mix 1 tablespoon butter and the thyme leaves. Arrange meat and onions on dinner plates; top meat with seasoned butter.

2 servings.

Tender, flavorful lamb is the basic meat of Greece and the Balkans. Thus, the exotic menu-mates. (Aside: The elegant broiler dessert is out of this world!)

MINT-GLAZED ROAST LAMB

Place roast fat side up on rack in shallow roasting pan. Season with salt and pepper before, during or after roasting (salt goes into roast only ¼ to ½ inch). Insert meat thermometer so tip is in thickest part of meat and does not touch bone or rest in fat.

Roast uncovered in 325° oven to desired doneness (see Timetable), using thermometer reading as final guide. During last hour of roasting, brush meat every 15 minutes with Mint Glaze (below). Serve any remaining glaze with roast.

Roasts are easier to carve if allowed to "set" 15 to 20 minutes after removing from oven. Since meat continues to cook after removal from oven, if roast is to set, it should be removed from oven when thermometer registers 5 to 10° lower than the desired doneness.

Mint Glaze

Heat ½ jar (10-ounce size) mint-flavored jelly, 1 clove garlic, crushed, and 2 teaspoons water, stirring constantly, until jelly is melted.

	TIMETABLE	
Cut	Approximate Cooking Time (Minutes per Lb.)	Meat Thermometer Reading
Rolled Leg 3 to 5 lbs.	35 to 40	175 to 180°
Leg 5 to 6 lbs.	30 to 35	175 to 180°
Square Shoulder 4 to 6 lbs.	30 to 35	175 to 180°

BULGUR PILAF

1 tablespoon finely chopped onion
1 tablespoon chopped green pepper
1 tablespoon butter or margarine
⅔ cup hot water
½ teaspoon instant chicken bouillon
⅓ cup bulgur wheat
1 can (2 ounces) sliced mushrooms, drained
¼ teaspoon salt
Dash pepper

In 8-inch skillet, cook and stir onion and green pepper in butter until onion is tender. Stir in remaining ingredients. Heat to boiling. Reduce heat; cover and simmer 10 minutes.

2 servings.

GOURMET PEARS

1 egg yolk*
3 tablespoons dairy sour cream
3 tablespoons granulated sugar
1 tablespoon rum, brandy or sherry
1 can (8 ounces) pears, drained
2 tablespoons brown sugar

In small saucepan, mix egg yolk, sour cream and granulated sugar. Cook, stirring constantly, until sauce is thickened, about 3 minutes. Cool. (Store in refrigerator if not using immediately.)

Stir rum into sour cream sauce. Place pears in 2 ungreased 6-ounce baking dishes or one 1¾-cup casserole. Pour sauce onto pears; sprinkle with brown sugar. Set oven control at broil and/or 550°. Broil with tops 6 to 8 inches from heat until brown sugar melts, 3 to 4 minutes. Serve hot or chilled.

2 servings.

*What about the egg white? Store in covered small container in refrigerator up to 3 days. Can be used for Individual Brownie Alaskas (page 8). Or add to whole eggs when preparing scrambled eggs.

Look-ahead lamb still has that international air. When the next time comes, go East or West—Chinese or American.

CHOPPED LAMB SANDWICH FILLING

½ cup chopped cooked lamb
2 tablespoons mayonnaise or
  salad dressing
3 tablespoons finely chopped celery
1½ teaspoons finely chopped onion
1 teaspoon prepared mustard

Mix all ingredients. Good on rye bread.

¾ cup (enough for 2 sandwiches).

CHINESE LAMB SUEY

2 tablespoons butter or margarine
1½ cups cooked lamb strips,
  2x¼x¼ inch
1 small onion, sliced and
  separated into rings
½ can (8-ounce size) water
  chestnuts, sliced*
¾ cup water
1 tablespoon soy sauce
1 tablespoon cornstarch
¾ teaspoon instant beef bouillon
½ teaspoon salt
1 package (6 ounces) frozen pea
  pods
  Hot cooked rice or chow mein
  noodles

Melt butter in 8-inch skillet; cook and stir meat and onion over medium heat until meat is brown and onion is tender. Add remaining ingredients except pea pods and rice. Heat to boiling, stirring occasionally. Add pea pods; cover and simmer 5 minutes. Serve on rice.

2 servings.

*Leftover water chestnuts? Slice and add to a crisp tossed green salad, chicken or tuna salad or cooked vegetable.

SHEPHERDS' PIE

Instant mashed potatoes
  (enough for 4 servings)
1 tablespoon parsley flakes or
  snipped parsley
1 envelope (about 1 ounce)
  gravy mix
1 cup cubed cooked lamb, beef or
  veal
2 tablespoons chopped onion
1 cup cooked vegetables (peas,
  carrots, corn, green beans)
¼ teaspoon salt

Heat oven to 350°. Prepare potatoes as directed on package except—stir in parsley flakes. Prepare gravy mix as directed.

In ungreased 1-quart casserole, mix gravy and remaining ingredients. Mound potatoes on meat mixture. Bake uncovered until potatoes are light brown, 25 to 30 minutes.

2 servings.

LAMB WITH DILL SAUCE

1 tablespoon butter or margarine
1 tablespoon flour
⅓ cup water
½ teaspoon instant chicken
  bouillon
2 tablespoons vinegar
½ teaspoon dill weed
  Salt and pepper
2 to 4 slices cooked lamb,
  ⅜ inch thick

Melt butter in small saucepan. Stir in flour. Cook over low heat, stirring until mixture is smooth and bubbly. Stir in water and bouillon. Heat to boiling, stirring constantly. Boil and stir 1 minute. Stir in vinegar and dill weed. Season with salt and pepper. Add meat and heat. Garnish with snipped parsley if desired.

2 servings.

Turkey more than meets the divide-and-conquer test. The way the bird comes now, the dividing is often already done for you. If you're a white meat buff or drumstick fan, just check the meat counter or frozen food section for turkey parts. Another good turkey buy for two is the handy rolled turkey roast. World's easiest carving. And so great for the sandwiches and salads on page 106. But if to you tradition means a whole turkey (as called for here), it's nice to know the smaller special has the identical anatomy as its big brother, so you can slice it up the very same way. (Just remember that for turkeys under 12 pounds, allow ¾ to 1 pound per serving.) And note the special touch to the tradition theme: a light pumpkin dessert—just right for two.

CELERY VICTOR

1 bunch celery
1 cup water
1 teaspoon instant beef bouillon
⅓ cup Italian dressing

Trim off root end of celery bunch but do not separate stalks. Remove leaves and coarse outer stalks; reserve some leaves for garnish. Cut celery bunch crosswise so bottom section is 3 inches long. (Refrigerate top section for future use.) Cut bottom section crosswise in half; tie halves with string.

In small saucepan, heat water and bouillon to boiling. Add celery halves; heat to boiling. Cover and cook until tender, about 15 minutes. Drain. Place celery halves in shallow 1-quart casserole; pour dressing on halves. Refrigerate 3 hours, spooning dressing on halves 2 or 3 times. Place celery half on each salad plate; remove string. Garnish with pimiento strips and celery leaves.

2 servings.

ROAST TURKEY

Choose a 4- to 8-pound fryer-roaster turkey. If turkey is frozen, thaw as directed on package. Wash turkey and pat dry.

If turkey is to be stuffed, stuff just before roasting. Use ½ package (7-ounce size) herbed stuffing and half the amounts of butter and water called for on package; prepare as directed. Fill wishbone area with stuffing first; fasten neck skin to back with skewer. Fold wings across back with tips touching. Fill body cavity lightly. (Do not pack—stuffing will expand while cooking.) Tuck drumsticks under band of skin at tail or tie together with heavy string, then tie to tail.

Place turkey breast side up on rack in shallow roasting pan. Brush with butter, salad oil or shortening. Insert meat thermometer so tip is in thickest part of inside thigh muscle or thickest part of breast meat and does not touch bone.

Roast uncovered in 325° oven, brushing occasionally with butter or pan drippings, until tender, 2½ to 3½ hours. If turkey is browning too quickly, cover loosely with aluminum foil. Meat thermometer should register 180 to 185°. Or test for doneness by pressing thickest part of the drumstick between protected fingers—if done, the meat should feel very soft. Or move drumstick up and down—if done, the joint should give readily or break.

When turkey is done, remove from oven and allow to stand about 20 minutes for easiest carving. Serve with Giblet Gravy (page 89) if you wish.

Remove every bit of stuffing from turkey as soon as possible after serving. Cool stuffing, meat and any gravy promptly; refrigerate separately. Use gravy or stuffing within 1 or 2 days; heat them thoroughly before serving. Serve cooked turkey meat within 2 or 3 days after roasting. If frozen, it can be kept up to 1 month.

GIBLET GRAVY

While turkey is roasting, cook giblets: In small saucepan, heat gizzard, heart, neck, ¼ teaspoon salt, 2 peppercorns, 1 bay leaf and enough water to cover to boiling. Reduce heat; cover and simmer until gizzard is fork tender, about 1 hour. Add liver during last 15 minutes of cooking. Remove meat from neck; finely chop giblets and reserve broth.

Pour drippings from roasting pan into bowl, leaving brown particles in pan. Return 1 tablespoon drippings to pan. Mix in 1 tablespoon flour. Cook over low heat, stirring until mixture is smooth and bubbly. Remove from heat. Stir in ½ cup of the reserved broth. Heat to boiling, stirring constantly. Boil and stir 1 minute. Stir in giblets and heat through.

About ¾ cup.

MASHED POTATOES

  3 medium potatoes (about 1 pound)
    About ¼ cup milk
  2 tablespoons soft butter or
    margarine
  ¼ teaspoon salt
    Dash pepper

Pare potatoes. Heat 1 inch salted water (½ teaspoon salt to 1 cup water) to boiling. Add potatoes. Cover and heat to boiling; cook until tender—30 to 35 minutes for whole potatoes, 20 to 25 minutes for cut. Drain. Gently shake pan over low heat to dry potatoes.

Mash potatoes until no lumps remain. Add milk in small amounts, beating after each addition. (Amount of milk needed to make potatoes smooth and fluffy depends on kind of potatoes.) Add butter, salt and pepper; beat until potatoes are light and fluffy. Dot with butter or sprinkle paprika or snipped parsley on top.

2 servings.

PUMPKIN CUSTARDS

  ½ can (16-ounce size) pumpkin
    pie mix*
  1 egg, slightly beaten
  ½ cup milk
    Streusel Topping (below)

Heat oven to 325°. Mix pie mix, egg and milk until smooth. Pour into 2 ungreased 10-ounce custard cups. Sprinkle Streusel Topping on top. Place cups in baking pan, 9x9x2 inches; pour very hot water into pan to within ½ inch of tops of cups.

Bake until knife inserted halfway between center and edge comes out clean, about 1 hour. Remove cups from water. Serve warm or chilled.

2 servings.

Streusel Topping

  ¼ cup brown sugar (packed)
  2 tablespoons flour
  2 tablespoons chopped pecans
  ¼ teaspoon cinnamon
  2 tablespoons soft butter or
    margarine

Mix all ingredients with fork until crumbly.

*Leftover pumpkin pie mix? Use in Frosty Pumpkin Custard (page 51).

Look what you can do for a turkey encore: salads, sandwiches, a quick one-dish dinner. Take off from there. Have fun!

HOT TURKEY SUPPER SALAD

1 cup cut-up cooked turkey
1 cup thinly sliced celery
½ cup croutons
½ cup mayonnaise
¼ cup diced roasted almonds
1 tablespoon lemon juice
1 teaspoon onion salt
¼ cup shredded Cheddar cheese
½ cup croutons or crushed potato chips

Heat oven to 350°. Mix all ingredients except cheese and ½ cup croutons. Divide between 2 ungreased 1½-cup casseroles. Sprinkle cheese and ½ cup croutons on tops. Bake 20 to 25 minutes.

2 servings.

BROILED TURKEY AND CHEESE SANDWICHES

1 package (10 ounces) frozen asparagus spears or broccoli spears
2 tablespoons deviled ham, if desired
2 slices toast, buttered
  Sliced cooked turkey
2 slices process American cheese

Cook asparagus spears as directed on package. Drain. Spread 1 tablespoon ham on each slice toast. Top with turkey slices, half the asparagus spears and a cheese slice.

Set oven control at broil and/or 550°. Broil sandwiches with tops 6 inches from heat just until cheese is bubbly, about 1 minute. Watch carefully!

2 servings.

TURKEY CREOLE

1 small onion, thinly sliced
½ small green pepper, cut into narrow strips
¼ cup thinly sliced celery
1 tablespoon salad oil
1 can (8 ounces) stewed tomatoes
1 can (8 ounces) tomato sauce
1 to 1½ teaspoons chili powder
¼ teaspoon salt
1½ cups cut-up cooked turkey
  Hot cooked rice or spaghetti

In 8-inch skillet, cook and stir onion, green pepper and celery in oil until vegetables are tender, about 5 minutes. Stir in tomatoes, tomato sauce, chili powder and salt; simmer uncovered 10 minutes. Stir in turkey; cover and simmer until turkey is hot, about 5 minutes. Serve on rice.

2 servings.

BACON-TURKEY CLUB SALAD

6 cups bite-size pieces lettuce
4 or 5 slices bacon, crisply fried and crumbled
1 medium tomato, cut into wedges
1½ cups cut-up cooked turkey
1 hard-cooked egg, sliced
  Barbecue Dressing (below)

Toss lettuce, bacon, tomato and turkey in bowl. Garnish with egg slices. Serve with dressing.

2 servings.

Barbecue Dressing

¼ cup mayonnaise or salad dressing
2 tablespoons barbecue sauce
2 teaspoons instant minced onion
2 teaspoons lemon juice
¼ teaspoon salt
⅛ teaspoon pepper

Mix all ingredients.

About ⅓ cup.

Pictured at right: Bacon-Turkey Club Salad, Broiled Turkey and Cheese Sandwiches and Turkey Creole

One of the great look-to-the-morrow roasts is pork. Fragrant and savory as it comes from the oven. Versatile thereafter. Enjoy this hearty dinner now and gird yourself for future pleasures.

**Roast Pork
Herbed Brussels Sprouts
Country-style Waldorf Salad
Yeast Rolls (page 80)
Lemon Pudding Cake**

ROAST PORK

Place roast fat side up on rack in shallow roasting pan. Season with salt and pepper before, during or after roasting (salt goes into roast only ¼ to ½ inch). Insert meat thermometer so tip is in center of thickest part of meat and does not touch bone or rest in fat.

Roast uncovered in 325° oven until done (see Timetable), using thermometer reading as final guide. Roasts are easier to carve if allowed to "set" 15 to 20 minutes after removing from oven. Since meat continues to cook after removal from oven, if roast is to set, it should be removed from oven when thermometer registers 5° lower than the desired doneness.

TIMETABLE

Cut	Approximate Cooking Time (Minutes per Lb.)	Meat Thermometer Reading
Loin		
Center		
3 to 5 lbs.	30 to 35	170°
Blade		
5 to 7 lbs.	35 to 40	170°
Sirloin		
3 to 4 lbs.	40 to 45	170°
Boneless Top (double)		
3 to 5 lbs.	35 to 45	170°
Boneless Top		
2 to 4 lbs.	30 to 35	170°

HERBED BRUSSELS SPROUTS

Cook 1 package (10 ounces) frozen Brussels sprouts as directed. Drain. Add 1 tablespoon butter or margarine and ⅛ teaspoon dill weed, caraway seed or marjoram leaves and toss.

2 servings.

COUNTRY-STYLE WALDORF SALAD

½ cup diced unpared apple (about ½ apple)
⅓ cup diced celery
¼ cup halved seedless green grapes
2 tablespoons coarsely chopped nuts
1 cup bite-size pieces lettuce
¼ cup mayonnaise or salad dressing

Toss all ingredients in bowl. Garnish salad with unpared apple slices.

2 servings.

LEMON PUDDING CAKE

1 egg, separated
1 teaspoon grated lemon peel
2 tablespoons lemon juice
⅓ cup milk
½ cup sugar
2 tablespoons flour
⅛ teaspoon salt

Heat oven to 325°. Beat egg white until stiff peaks form. Beat egg yolk; add remaining ingredients and beat until smooth. Fold in egg white.

Divide between ungreased 1-cup baking dishes or 6-ounce custard cups. Place in pan of hot water (1 inch deep). Bake 45 to 50 minutes. Serve warm, with whipped cream if you like.

2 generous servings.

Applause from the audience as pork stages a comeback. Star it in an Oriental show of chow mein or a speedy meal-in-a-skillet. And for a final bow, a casserole that calls for your can opener and oven to do most of the work.

PORK CHOW MEIN

1 tablespoon salad oil or
   shortening
1 to 1½ cups cubed cooked pork
1 small onion, chopped (about ¼
   cup)
1 cup water
1 teaspoon instant chicken bouillon
¼ teaspoon garlic salt
1 can (about 3 ounces) sliced
   mushrooms, drained (reserve
   liquid)
1 tablespoon soy sauce
2 tablespoons cornstarch
1 can (16 ounces) Chinese
   vegetables, drained
   Chow mein noodles

Heat oil in 8-inch skillet; brown meat and push to one side. Add onion; cook and stir until onion is tender. Stir in water, bouillon and garlic salt; heat to boiling. Reduce heat; cover and simmer 5 minutes.

Blend reserved mushroom liquid, soy sauce and cornstarch; stir into meat mixture. Add mushrooms and Chinese vegetables. Cook, stirring constantly, until mixture thickens and boils. Boil and stir 1 minute. Serve on noodles, and if you like, with additional soy sauce.

2 servings.

Variations

Beef, Chicken or Turkey Chow Mein: Substitute 1 to 1½ cups cubed cooked beef, chicken or turkey for the pork.

CHINESE PORK AND RICE

⅓ cup uncooked regular rice
¼ cup chopped onion
1 stalk celery, cut into diagonal
   slices
1 tablespoon salad oil
¾ cup water
1 teaspoon instant chicken or beef
   bouillon
1 tablespoon soy sauce
1 cup cut-up cooked pork (¾-inch
   pieces)
½ green pepper, chopped

In 8-inch skillet, cook and stir rice, onion and celery in oil over medium heat until rice is golden brown and onion is tender. Stir in water, bouillon, soy sauce and meat; heat to boiling, stirring occasionally. Reduce heat; cover tightly and simmer until rice is tender, 12 to 15 minutes. Stir in green pepper; cover and simmer until liquid is absorbed and pepper is crisp-tender, about 5 minutes.

2 servings.

SAUCY PORK 'N NOODLE BAKE

1 tablespoon salad oil
1 cup cut-up cooked pork
½ cup uncooked noodles
1 can (10½ ounces) condensed
   cream of chicken soup
1 can (8 ounces) whole kernel
   corn, drained
1 tablespoon sliced pimiento
½ cup shredded sharp Cheddar
   cheese
¼ cup finely diced green pepper

Heat oven to 375°. Heat oil in 8-inch skillet; brown meat over medium-high heat. Drain off fat. Stir in remaining ingredients. Pour into ungreased 1-quart casserole. Bake uncovered until noodles are tender, about 45 minutes.

2 generous servings.

Something Special...

Freezing Tips

Freezing ABC's

Hurry! Moving fast is the first secret of successful freezing. Cool cooked foods quickly (small amounts in the refrigerator, larger portions in a bowl of ice and water). Then wrap and rush to the freezer. Hurry home with the frozens you buy. For anything frozen or to-be-frozen, the zero hour is now!

Pack properly. It's critical. Any already-frozen food can be transferred to your own freezer without rewrapping. But if you're starting from scratch, be sure to use the wraps that are specially designed for freezing. Wrap tightly, pressing out all air; seal with tape. Or easier, use heavy-duty freezer bags. Again, press out air bubbles and seal securely with twist closures. If you use freezer containers (for stews, casseroles and the like), allow plenty of headspace. Food expands in freezing.

Identify. Use a felt pen or grease pencil to note the following on freezer tape:
• What's in the package
• Date by which it should be used

Freeze at zero . . . or below. The lower the temperature, the faster foods freeze. And the faster they freeze, the less apt they are to lose flavor and texture. An even, low temperature is also a must for *keeping* foods in prime condition.

Freezing for Two

Extras. No matter how smartly you shop, cooking for two always seems to produce an excess bit of this or that. For short-term storage, use little see-through plastic bags to freeze dabs of chopped onion, chopped green pepper, drained pimiento, nuts, grated cheese, grated peels—and put those leftovers to work.

Excesses. Plan around them. Cook a big piece of meat. Cool the leftovers quickly. Cover and refrigerate right away (to use within 1 or 2 days). Or freeze in meal-size portions: Most cooked meats and poultry can be frozen up to 1 month—up to 6 months if frozen with broth or gravy. Allow to thaw (still freezer-wrapped) in the refrigerator. See recipes in this chapter for ways to use leftover meat. For specifics on uncooked meat, poultry and fish, see pages 114–117.

Stews, Chili and Sauces

Before freezing: Do not overcook. Keep spice level low. Avoid potatoes—they don't freeze well. Cool quickly. Leave headspace in container to allow for expansion.

Maximum storage: 3 to 4 months.

To reheat: Heat slowly in saucepan 20 to 30 minutes, stirring occasionally; add liquid if necessary.

Breads

Before freezing: Wrap rolls and French bread in meal-size portions. (French bread can be sliced and buttered first.) Bakery bread can be frozen in its store wrap—overwrap if it is to be stored longer than 3 months. (A slice of bread will thaw in 10 minutes).

Maximum storage: 2 to 3 months for biscuits, muffins, nut breads (quick breads); 9 months for yeast breads and rolls.

To reheat: Leave in foil wrap and heat in 350° oven (20 to 25 minutes if frozen, 10 minutes if thawed). Frozen sliced bread can be toasted.

Cakes and Cupcakes

Before freezing: Wrap whole or in serving pieces. (Frozen cake can be sliced easily.) Freeze frosted cakes uncovered, then wrap.

Maximum storage: 2 to 3 months if frosted; 4 to 6 months if unfrosted.

To thaw: Leave in freezer wrap. Let unfrosted cakes stand at room temperature 2 to 3 hours (about 30 minutes for cupcakes); place frosted cakes, loosely covered, in refrigerator.

Cookies

Before freezing: Place cool cookies in airtight container or freezer wrap.

Maximum storage: 9 to 12 months.

To thaw: Let cookies stand at room temperature.

TWO IS COMPANY

Memory-making dinners that say, "Tonight is special"

HERB-ROASTED CHICKEN

2½- to 3-pound broiler-fryer chicken
¼ cup butter or margarine, melted
¼ teaspoon rosemary
¼ teaspoon thyme
¼ teaspoon marjoram
  Parsleyed Mixed Vegetables
  (below)
  Parsley

Heat oven to 375°. Rub cavity of chicken with salt if desired. Place chicken breast side up on rack in roasting pan. Mix butter, rosemary, thyme and marjoram; brush half the herb-butter mixture on chicken. Roast uncovered until done, 1¼ to 1¾ hours, brushing chicken with remaining herb-butter mixture several times. If chicken is browning too quickly, cover loosely with aluminum foil. Chicken is done when drumstick meat feels very soft when pressed. Place chicken on heated platter; surround with vegetables and garnish with parsley.

2 servings.

Parsleyed Mixed Vegetables

4 small or 2 medium potatoes,
  pared
2 medium carrots, cut lengthwise
  into halves
2 small onions
½ teaspoon seasoned salt
¼ cup water or chicken broth
2 small zucchini, cut lengthwise
  into quarters
½ teaspoon seasoned salt
  Snipped parsley

Heat oven to 375°. If using medium potatoes, cut each in half. Combine all ingredients except zucchini, ½ teaspoon seasoned salt and the parsley in ungreased 1-quart casserole. Cover and bake 50 minutes. Add zucchini and salt; bake until vegetables are done, about 10 minutes. Arrange vegetables on platter; spoon on some liquid and sprinkle with parsley.

2 servings.

CRÊPES SUZETTE

  Crêpes (below)
¼ cup butter or margarine
¼ teaspoon grated orange peel
¼ cup orange juice
1 tablespoon sugar
2 tablespoons orange-flavored
  liqueur or 2 tablespoons brandy

Prepare Crêpes. In 8-inch skillet, heat butter, orange peel, orange juice and sugar to boiling, stirring occasionally. Boil and stir 1 minute. Reduce heat. Fold crêpes into fourths; place in hot orange sauce, turning crêpes once.

To flame, heat orange-flavored liqueur just until warm in long-handled ladle or small pan. Ignite and pour flaming over crêpes in skillet. Place 2 crêpes on each dessert plate; spoon sauce on crêpes.

2 servings.

Crêpes

½ cup all-purpose flour
1 teaspoon sugar
¼ teaspoon baking powder
¼ teaspoon salt
⅔ cup milk
1 egg
¼ teaspoon vanilla
2 teaspoons butter or margarine,
  melted

Beat all ingredients with rotary beater until smooth. For each crêpe, lightly butter 8-inch skillet; heat over medium heat until butter is bubbly. Pour scant ¼ cup batter into skillet; immediately rotate pan until batter covers bottom. Cook until light brown; turn and brown other side. Stack crêpes so first-baked side is down. Cool, keeping crêpes covered to prevent them from drying out.

4 to 6 crêpes.

As soon as you pour the crêpe batter into the skillet, quickly rotate the pan so that the batter covers the bottom evenly.

The tissue-thin crêpe can be lifted easily. Check the color of the bottom to see if it's time to turn it—it should be light brown.

Dim the lights, then bring out the crêpes in their orange sauce and flame them at the table for a triumphant finale to your dinner.

A windfall! Maybe that tax refund finally showed up. Or Uncle Max decided to give you his old car. Occasions enough to link arms in a lively Zorba the Greek dance and enjoy this sophisticated but quickly put-together dinner. The salad is virtually a celebration in and of itself. Whether you first encounter the distinctive tang and texture of feta while traveling on the Isles or shopping down the aisles, you'll appreciate it in tandem with Bibb lettuce.

Lamb Shish Kabobs
Parsleyed Rice
Greek Salad
Sesame Hard Rolls
Raspberry Crème
Almond Cookies

LAMB SHISH KABOBS

¾ pound boneless lamb shoulder, cut into 1-inch cubes
¼ cup Caesar dressing or French dressing
1 can (8 ounces) whole onions, drained
  About 8 pineapple chunks
  Green pepper pieces (½ pepper)
  Red pepper pieces (½ pepper)
  Parsleyed Rice (below)

Place meat in glass bowl; pour dressing on meat. Cover and refrigerate at least 8 hours.

Remove meat from marinade; reserve marinade. Alternate meat cubes, onions, pineapple chunks and green and red pepper pieces on each of 4 skewers. Set oven control at broil and/or 550°. Place skewers on rack in broiler pan. Brush some of the reserved marinade on kabobs. Broil with tops 4 to 5 inches from heat until meat is brown, about 6 minutes. Turn; brush remaining marinade on kabobs. Broil until done, about 5 minutes. Serve kabobs on Parsleyed Rice.

2 servings.

Parsleyed Rice

Cook instant rice as directed on package for 2 servings. Stir in 1 tablespoon snipped parsley.

GREEK SALAD

2 small heads Bibb lettuce
1 medium tomato, cut into wedges
6 pitted ripe olives
⅛ teaspoon oregano
1 tablespoon crumbled feta cheese or blue cheese
  Lemon-Oil Dressing (below)
  Lemon wedges

Place 1 head Bibb lettuce on each salad plate. Arrange tomato wedges and olives between leaves. Sprinkle oregano and cheese on salads; drizzle with dressing. Garnish salads with lemon wedges.

2 servings.

Lemon-Oil Dressing

¼ cup olive oil or salad oil
1 tablespoon lemon juice
⅛ teaspoon salt
  Dash pepper

Shake all ingredients in tightly covered jar.

About ¼ cup.

RASPBERRY CRÈME

Mix 1 carton (8 ounces) raspberry yogurt and ½ cup frozen whipped topping (thawed). Divide between dessert dishes. Top with a dollop of whipped topping and garnish with mint leaves.

2 servings.

COQ AU VIN

 3 slices bacon
¼ cup all-purpose flour
½ teaspoon salt
⅛ teaspoon pepper
1½ pounds chicken pieces
   (legs, thighs, breasts)
¼ pound fresh mushrooms, sliced
 2 small onions, cut into halves
 2 carrots, cut diagonally into
   2-inch pieces
 1 teaspoon instant chicken
   bouillon or 1 chicken bouillon
   cube
½ teaspoon Italian herb seasoning
   or ⅛ teaspoon each thyme,
   basil, marjoram and sage
¾ cup water
½ cup red Burgundy
   Snipped parsley

In Dutch oven or 3-quart saucepan, fry bacon until crisp; remove and drain. Mix flour, salt and pepper in plastic or paper bag. Shake chicken, 2 or 3 pieces at a time, in bag until coated. Brown chicken in bacon fat; remove to warm platter.

Cook and stir mushrooms and onion in Dutch oven until onion is tender. Drain off fat. Place chicken in Dutch oven; crumble bacon on chicken and add remaining ingredients except parsley. Heat to boiling. Reduce heat; cover and simmer until thickest chicken pieces are tender, about 30 minutes. Sprinkle parsley on top.

2 servings.

Time-saver: You can substitute canned vegetables for the fresh. Use 1 jar (2 ounces) button mushrooms, 1 can (8¾ ounces) small onions and 1 can (8 ounces) whole carrots. Drain and reserve liquids. Add enough water to reserved vegetable liquids to measure ¾ cup. Substitute this liquid for the ¾ cup water. Add canned vegetables after chicken has simmered and is tender; heat through, about 10 minutes.

TOSSED ROMAINE SALAD

 3 cups bite-size pieces romaine
   (1 small head)
 4 or 5 radishes, sliced
 2 tablespoons salad oil
 1 tablespoon wine, tarragon
   or cider vinegar
 1 small clove garlic, crushed, or
   ⅛ teaspoon garlic powder
¼ teaspoon salt
   Dash pepper

Combine romaine and radish slices in bowl. Mix remaining ingredients; pour onto vegetables and toss.

2 servings.

POTS DE CRÈME AU CHOCOLAT

½ bar (4-ounce size) sweet cooking
   chocolate
 1 tablespoon sugar
⅓ cup light cream (20%) or half-and-half
 1 egg yolk, slightly beaten
¼ teaspoon vanilla

In small saucepan, cook chocolate, sugar and cream over medium heat, stirring constantly, until chocolate is melted and mixture is smooth. Remove from heat; beat into egg yolk. Stir in vanilla. Pour into pots de crème cups, demitasse cups or other small dessert dishes. Chill. If you like, serve with whipped cream and garnish with mint leaf.

2 servings.

**Coq au Vin
Tossed Romaine Salad
Crusty French Bread
Pots de Crème
au Chocolat**

BROILED SIRLOIN STEAK

1- to 1½-pound beef sirloin steak,
  1 to 1½ inches thick

Set oven control at broil and/or 550°. Diagonally slash outer edge of fat on steak at 1-inch intervals to prevent curling (do not cut into lean). Broil steak with top 3 to 5 inches from heat to desired doneness, 6 to 8 minutes on each side for rare, 8 to 10 minutes for medium. Test for doneness by cutting a small slit near center of meat. Season steak *after* browning. (Salt tends to draw moisture to surface and delay browning.) Serve immediately.

2 servings.

Note: Use this method for broiling top loin, porterhouse, T-bone, rib or rib eye steaks.

EASY HASH BROWNS WITH ONIONS

½ package (6-ounce size) hash
  brown potatoes with onions*
⅔ cup water
½ teaspoon salt
2 tablespoons butter or margarine

In 8-inch skillet, combine half the potatoes, the water, salt and butter. Cook uncovered over medium-high heat until liquid is absorbed and potatoes are brown on bottom, 8 to 10 minutes. Turn with pancake turner and cook until brown on bottom, about 3 minutes.

2 servings.

*To use half the package, measure contents and divide in half (approximately 1 cup). To store remaining mix, close package securely and use within 2 weeks. Serve again with scrambled eggs, chops or broiled chicken.

GOURMET TOSSED SALAD

2½ cups bite-size pieces crisp salad
  greens
½ cup sliced fresh mushrooms
½ cup small cauliflowerets
2 tablespoons chopped green
  pepper
1 to 2 tablespoons crumbled blue
  cheese
  Oil-and-Vinegar Dressing
  (page 62)
  Thinly sliced onion rings
  Pimiento-stuffed olive slices

Toss salad greens, mushrooms, cauliflowerets, green pepper, cheese and dressing in bowl. Garnish with onion rings and olive slices.

2 servings.

APPLE PIE

  Pastry for 8-inch two-crust pie
  (facing page)
½ cup sugar
3 tablespoons flour
¼ teaspoon nutmeg
¼ teaspoon cinnamon
  Dash salt
5 cups thinly sliced pared tart
  apples (about 5 medium)
1 tablespoon butter or margarine

Prepare pastry. Mix sugar, flour, nutmeg, cinnamon and salt; pour on apples and toss. Turn filling into pastry-lined pie pan and dot with butter.

Heat oven to 425°. Cover filling with top crust which has slits cut in it; seal and flute. Cover edge with 2- to 3-inch-wide strip of aluminum foil to prevent excessive browning; remove foil last 15 minutes of baking. Bake until crust is golden brown and juice begins to bubble through crust, 40 to 50 minutes. Cool slightly on wire rack. Serve warm, with cinnamon ice cream or Cheddar cheese if you like.

Broiled Sirloin Steak
Easy Hash Browns with Onions
Gourmet Tossed Salad
Warm Apple Pie with Cinnamon Ice Cream

Into mixing bowl, measure **1½ cups all-purpose flour** and **¾ teaspoon salt** (if using self-rising flour, omit salt). Cut in **½ cup plus 2 tablespoons shortening**. Sprinkle in **3 tablespoons water** gradually, mixing with fork until all flour is moistened. Shape dough firmly into ball. Divide dough in half; shape one half into flattened round on lightly floured cloth-covered board.

Roll dough 1½ inches larger all around than pie pan, using stockinet-covered rolling pin. Carefully lift dough occasionally; if it sticks, rub a little flour into cloth beneath and continue rolling. Ease pastry into 8-inch pie pan. Turn filling into pan. Trim overhanging edge of pastry ½ inch from rim of pan with kitchen scissors. Shape remaining half of dough into flattened round and roll 2 inches larger all around than pie pan.

Cut slits in pastry; place on filling. Trim overhanging edge of pastry 1 inch from rim of pan. Fold and roll top edge of pastry under lower edge, pressing on rim to seal; flute. Cover edge of crust with 2- to 3-inch-wide strip of aluminum foil to prevent excessive browning during baking; remove foil for last 15 minutes of baking. Bake pie as directed in recipe.

Cut shortening into flour with pastry blender, using a rocking motion, until mixture looks like coarse crumbs.

Shape dough firmly into a ball when all flour is moistened and dough leaves side of bowl almost clean.

Roll with light strokes from the center outward, lifting rolling pin as you reach edge so dough does not become too thin.

Roll dough into circle 1½ inches larger all around than inverted pie pan, then fold into quarters, place in pan, unfold and ease in.

Fold pastry into quarters; cut 4 slits in each fold to allow steam to escape during baking. Place pastry on filling and unfold.

Fold and roll top edge of crust under lower edge. Flute; for a more definitive shape, repinch around handle of knife.

Something Special...

Pastry for Pies

Full moon? In the Orient that's cause for celebration. So why not make moon time your special time, too? Put the pork in the spotlight on a table by a window; Chinese pea pods, carrot and cucumber sticks and a melon dessert complete this Eastern inspiration. Sit there, feast and set your gaze.

Sweet-and-Sour Pork
Fluffy White Rice
Chinese Pea Pods
Carrot Sticks
Cucumber Sticks
Melon Boats with Sherbet

SWEET-AND-SOUR PORK

    Salad oil
    Sweet-and-Sour Sauce (right)
½ cup all-purpose flour
¼ cup cornstarch
1 teaspoon salt
¼ teaspoon monosodium glutamate
½ teaspoon baking powder
½ cup water
1 teaspoon salad oil
½ pound pork tenderloin, cut into ¼-inch slices
1 medium green pepper, cut into 1-inch pieces
1 small onion, cut into 1-inch pieces
1½ cups hot cooked rice

Pour oil into electric skillet or large saucepan to depth of 1 to 1½ inches. Heat to 375°, or until 1-inch bread cube browns in 1 minute. While oil heats, prepare Sweet-and-Sour Sauce.

In small bowl, beat flour, cornstarch, salt, monosodium glutamate, baking powder, water and 1 teaspoon oil with rotary beater until smooth. Dip meat into batter with tongs; fry in hot oil, turning once, until golden brown, 6 to 8 minutes. Drain; keep warm.

Stir green pepper and onion into Sweet-and-Sour Sauce. Cover and simmer until vegetables are crisp-tender, about 5 minutes. Serve meat and sauce on rice.

2 servings.

Sweet-and-Sour Sauce

¼ cup brown sugar (packed)
2 tablespoons cornstarch
1 can (8¼ ounces) pineapple chunks, drained (reserve syrup)
¼ cup vinegar
2 tablespoons catsup

In 2-quart saucepan, mix sugar and cornstarch. Add enough water to reserved pineapple syrup to measure 1 cup. Stir syrup mixture, vinegar and catsup into cornstarch mixture. Cook, stirring constantly, until mixture thickens and boils. Stir in pineapple. Keep warm over very low heat.

MELON BOATS WITH SHERBET

Top wedges of chilled honeydew melon or cantaloupe with scoops of lemon or lime sherbet.

Note: Melon out of season? Use 1 package (12 ounces) frozen melon balls, partially thawed, instead.

Something to Know About...

Use tongs to dip each piece of pork into the batter; fry each piece as you've battered it. The pork will be easier to slice thin if it's partially frozen.

So you have a good and proper reason to splurge—but the checkbook says, "Not tonight, fellas!" What do you do? You work wonders with a bit of round steak. You take time (and a mix) to make a crunchy-topped hot bread. Then finish on a high note with a dazzle of a dessert.

CURRIED BEEF AND PEPPERS

½ to ¾ pound beef round steak
2 tablespoons salad oil
1 beef bouillon cube
1¼ cups water
1 teaspoon sugar, if desired
1 teaspoon curry powder
½ teaspoon salt
1 small green pepper, cut into 1-inch pieces
1 medium onion, cut into wedges
2 tablespoons cornstarch
2 tablespoons water
1 tomato, peeled and cut into wedges
Buttered noodles

Cut meat into ¾-inch pieces. Heat oil in 8-inch skillet; brown meat over medium heat, about 10 minutes. Drain off fat.

Add bouillon cube, 1¼ cups water, the sugar, curry powder and salt; heat to boiling, stirring occasionally. Reduce heat; cover and simmer until meat is tender, about 1 hour. (Add small amount water if necessary.)

Add green pepper and onion; cover and simmer until vegetables are crisp-tender, about 5 minutes. Mix cornstarch and 2 tablespoons water; stir into meat and vegetable mixture. Cook over medium heat, stirring constantly, until sauce is clear and bubbly, about 1 minute. Add tomato wedges; cover and cook over low heat until tomatoes are hot, about 3 minutes. Serve on noodles.

2 servings.

QUICK SESAME BREAD

1 cup buttermilk baking mix
¼ cup water
2 teaspoons soft butter or margarine
1 tablespoon sesame seed

Heat oven to 400°. Stir baking mix and water with fork to a soft dough. On greased baking sheet, spread or roll dough into rectangle, 6x4 inches. Brush butter on rectangle; sprinkle with sesame seed. Bake until golden brown, 8 to 10 minutes. Serve hot, broken into pieces or cut into squares.

2 servings.

FRUIT MEDLEY

Choose two or more of the following fruits to total 1 to 1½ cups: seedless green grapes; strawberries; banana slices; peach, pear or pineapple chunks; mandarin orange segments; dark sweet cherries. Divide between dessert dishes; sprinkle snipped fresh mint on fruit if desired. Serve with one of the toppings below.

2 servings.

Honey-Yogurt Topping

Mix 1 tablespoon lemon juice, 1 tablespoon honey and ½ cup unflavored yogurt or dairy sour cream.

Brown Sugar-Yogurt Topping

Mix ¼ cup unflavored yogurt or dairy sour cream and 2 tablespoons brown sugar.

Limeade-Yogurt Topping

Mix 2 tablespoons frozen limeade concentrate (thawed) and ¼ cup pineapple yogurt.

Spice-Yogurt Topping

Mix ½ cup unflavored yogurt or dairy sour cream, 1 tablespoon sugar, ¼ teaspoon cinnamon and dash nutmeg.

Curried Beef and Peppers
Buttered Noodles
Lettuce Wedges with Oil-and-Vinegar Dressing
Quick Sesame Bread
Fruit Medley

ROAST CORNISH HENS

2 Rock Cornish hens (about 1
  pound each)
  Salt
¼ cup soft butter or margarine
¼ teaspoon red pepper sauce or
  ½ teaspoon thyme, marjoram or
  tarragon leaves
  Preserved kumquats
  Watercress

Thaw hens if frozen. Heat oven to 350°.
Rub cavities of hens with salt if desired.
Place hens breast side up on rack in shallow roasting pan. Mix butter and red pepper sauce. Brush part of butter mixture on hens and sprinkle with salt. Roast uncovered until tender, about 1 hour, brushing hens 3 or 4 times with remaining butter mixture. Garnish with preserved kumquats and watercress.

2 servings.

WILD RICE WITH MUSHROOMS AND ALMONDS

2 tablespoons butter or margarine
⅓ cup uncooked wild rice
1 tablespoon slivered almonds
1 tablespoon chopped onion
1 can (2 ounces) mushroom stems
  and pieces
1 cup chicken broth*

Melt butter in 8-inch skillet; cook and stir rice, almonds and onion until almonds are golden brown, about 10 minutes.

Heat oven to 350°. Stir mushrooms (with liquid) and chicken broth into skillet; heat to boiling. Pour rice mixture into ungreased 2½-cup casserole. Cover and bake until all liquid is absorbed and rice is tender, about 1 hour.

2 servings.

*Chicken broth can be made by dissolving 1 chicken bouillon cube or 1 teaspoon instant chicken bouillon in 1 cup boiling water.

ARTICHOKES WITH LEMON BUTTER

1½ quarts water
 1 tablespoon lemon juice
 ½ teaspoon salt
 2 artichokes
   Lemon Butter (below)

In 3-quart saucepan, heat water, lemon juice and salt to boiling. Remove discolored leaves and the small leaves at base of each artichoke. Trim stem even with base of artichoke. Cut 1 inch off top and discard top. Snip off points of remaining leaves with scissors. Tie each artichoke with string around side and from top to bottom to hold leaves in place. Place artichokes in saucepan; heat to boiling.

Reduce heat; cover and simmer until done, 30 to 40 minutes. (Artichokes are done when leaves pull off easily and bottom is tender when pierced with knife.) Remove artichokes with tongs or 2 large spoons; place upside down to drain. Remove string and serve upright. Serve hot with Lemon Butter.

2 servings.

Lemon Butter

Heat ¼ cup butter or margarine, 1 teaspoon grated lemon peel and 2 tablespoons lemon juice over low heat until butter is melted.

About ⅓ cup.

Note: To eat artichokes, pull off leaves one at a time. Dip base of leaf into Lemon Butter; turn leaf meaty side down and draw between teeth, scraping off meat portion. Discard leaf on plate. When all leaves have been removed, cut off the spiny choke and eat the smooth round bottom portion—a great delicacy.

ORIENTAL FONDUE

Choose one to three of the following meats and seafoods to total ¾ pound:

Pork tenderloin, cut into ⅛-inch
   slices
Chicken breasts, boned and cut
   across grain into bite-size slices
   (about ¼ inch thick)
Frozen scallops, thawed and cut
   into ¾-inch pieces
Cleaned raw shrimp, fresh or
   frozen*

Choose three or four of the following vegetables:

¼ cauliflower, separated into
   flowerets
¼ pound broccoli, separated into
   flowerets
½ package (10-ounce size) frozen
   Chinese pea pods
2 medium carrots, cut diagonally
   into ⅛-inch slices
¼ pound fresh mushrooms,
   thinly sliced
1 bunch green onions (about 6),
   cut into ½-inch lengths

And have ready:

8 cups chicken broth**
1½ cups hot cooked rice
   Choice of dipping sauces (right)

Arrange meat, seafood and vegetables on tray or platter; garnish with parsley. Cover and refrigerate until serving time.

Pour chicken broth into 10-inch electric skillet, metal fondue pot or chafing dish until about ⅔ full (add any remaining chicken broth as needed); heat to simmering. Divide rice between 2 small bowls. Serve dipping sauces in small bowls.

Each person uses chopsticks or fondue forks to place an assortment of meat and vegetables (2 or 3 pieces at a time) in broth. Cook foods until done, 2 to 4 minutes; transfer to dinner plate and dip into a sauce. After the main course, ladle broth on remaining rice in bowls and eat as soup.

2 servings.

Note: Meat will slice easier if partially frozen.

*Rinse frozen shrimp under running cold water to remove ice glaze.
**4 cans (13¾ ounces each) chicken broth and 1 cup water or 3 cans (10½ ounces each) condensed chicken broth, diluted as directed.

Lemon-Soy Sauce

¼ cup lemon juice
¼ cup soy sauce
2 tablespoons sweet sake (for
   cooking) or sherry

Mix all ingredients.

About ½ cup.

Sweet-and-Sour Sauce

2 tablespoons brown sugar
1 teaspoon cornstarch
2 tablespoons cider vinegar
⅓ cup pineapple juice
1 tablespoon catsup

Mix all ingredients in small saucepan. Cook over medium-high heat, stirring constantly, until mixture thickens and boils. Boil and stir 1 minute.

About ½ cup.

Plum Sauce

¼ cup chili sauce
¼ cup plum jam or grape jelly
¼ teaspoon hot sauce

Mix all ingredients.

About ½ cup.

Hot Mustard Sauce

3 tablespoons dry mustard
2 tablespoons water

Mix ingredients.

About ¼ cup.

Oriental Fondue
Fluffy White Rice
Kumquats
Almond Cookies
Tea

SHRIMP CURRY

Condiments (below)
1 can (10½ ounces) condensed
cream of shrimp soup
1 teaspoon parsley flakes
¾ teaspoon curry powder
1 tablespoon instant minced onion
12 ounces frozen cleaned raw
shrimp*
Green Rice (right)

Prepare Condiments. In medium saucepan, heat soup, parsley flakes, curry powder and onion to boiling, stirring occasionally. Stir in shrimp; heat to boiling. Reduce heat; cover and simmer until shrimp are done, about 10 minutes. Serve curry with Green Rice.

2 servings.

*Rinse frozen shrimp under running cold water to remove ice glaze.

Condiments

Choose three to six of the following:
Diced tomatoes
Golden raisins
Toasted shredded coconut
Chopped hard-cooked eggs
Sweet pickle sticks
Chutney
Kumquats
Chopped green pepper
Grated orange peel
Grated lemon peel
Salted diced almonds
Currant jelly
Peeled and sliced avocado

Shrimp Curry
Condiments
Green Rice
Sesame Crackers
Baked Banana with
Butter Pecan Ice Cream
Spiced Tea

Green Rice

⅔ cup uncooked regular rice
½ cup chopped fresh spinach
leaves
2 teaspoons instant minced onion
1 tablespoon butter or margarine
1 teaspoon salt
1⅓ cups boiling water

Heat oven to 350°. Mix all ingredients in ungreased 1-quart casserole. Cover and bake until liquid is absorbed and rice is tender, about 30 minutes.

2 servings.

BAKED BANANA

Heat oven to 350°. Cut peeled large banana lengthwise in half. Place halves cut sides down in greased baking dish and brush with lemon juice.

Drizzle with 1 tablespoon butter or margarine, melted, and if desired, 2 teaspoons light rum or ¼ teaspoon rum flavoring. Sprinkle 1 teaspoon grated lemon peel and 2 teaspoons brown sugar on top. Bake uncovered 20 minutes. Serve warm with butter pecan ice cream or any favorite flavor.

2 servings.

SPICED TEA

2 tea bags
3 whole cloves, broken into pieces
¼ teaspoon dried orange peel
⅛ teaspoon cinnamon
2 cups boiling water

In heated teapot or other heatproof container, place tea bags, cloves, orange peel and cinnamon. Pour boiling water into teapot. Cover and steep 3 to 5 minutes. Stir just before serving.

2 servings.

A raise in pay? A small spree is in order. For inspiration, flip back to the picture on page 95—a spectacular main dish if ever there was one. Don't miss the chance to present it proudly before you take it back to the kitchen to cut it up. Note the choice of vegetables, too—both easy but elegant. The make-ahead dessert is one to remember for party meals. Just double (or triple) syrup and liqueur.

DUCKLING À L'ORANGE

4- to 5-pound duckling
2 tablespoons butter or margarine
2 tablespoons finely chopped onion
¼ teaspoon tarragon leaves
1½ tablespoons shredded orange peel
½ cup orange juice
¼ teaspoon salt
⅛ teaspoon dry mustard
¼ cup currant jelly
2 tablespoons port or cranberry cocktail
1 teaspoon cornstarch

Fasten neck skin of duckling with skewers. Lift wing tips up and over back for natural brace. Heat oven to 325°. Place duckling breast side up on rack in shallow roasting pan.

Melt butter in small saucepan. Cook and stir onion and tarragon leaves in butter until onion is tender. Add orange peel, orange juice, salt, mustard, jelly and port; cook and stir over medium heat until jelly is melted.

Measure orange sauce; reserve half the sauce to serve with duckling. Brush duckling with part of remaining orange sauce. Roast uncovered until done, about 2½ hours, pricking skin with fork and brushing occasionally with remaining orange sauce. If duckling is browning too quickly, cover loosely with aluminum foil. Duckling is done when drumstick meat feels very soft when pressed.

In small saucepan, mix reserved orange sauce and the cornstarch. Cook over medium heat, stirring constantly, until mixture boils. Boil and stir 1 minute. Serve sauce in small pitcher. Remove duckling to warm platter; garnish with watercress, orange twists, grapes or kumquats.

2 servings.

Something to Know About...

To serve the duckling after you've presented it at the table, cut it lengthwise in half. Keep close to the top of the wishbone and the center of the back. Then cut each half into 2 pieces. (Poultry shears work best for this, but you can also use kitchen shears or a sharp, sturdy knife.)

BARLEY PILAF

1 tablespoon butter or margarine
⅓ cup uncooked barley
1 tablespoon instant minced onion
1 teaspoon instant chicken bouillon
¼ teaspoon celery salt
⅛ teaspoon pepper
1 cup boiling water
1 tablespoon snipped parsley

Heat oven to 325°. In ungreased 2½-cup casserole, mix all ingredients except parsley. Cover and bake until done, about 1 hour. Stir in parsley.

2 servings.

MUSHROOM GREEN BEANS

1 can (2 ounces) mushroom stems
  and pieces, drained (reserve
  liquid)
½ package (10-ounce size) frozen
  French-style green beans*
¼ teaspoon salt
1 teaspoon butter or margarine

Add enough water to reserved mushroom liquid to measure ¼ cup; pour into small saucepan. Add beans and salt. Cover and cook until tender, about 5 minutes. Drain. Stir in butter and mushrooms; heat through.

2 servings.

*Leftover frozen green beans? Use in Deep-dish Hamburger Pie (page 36).

SPINACH SOUFFLÉ

Heat oven to 325°. Remove frozen spinach soufflé (12-ounce size) from container. Cut into quarters. Place 2 quarters in each of 2 ungreased 10-ounce baking dishes, overlapping quarters if necessary. Bake until knife inserted in center comes out clean, 50 to 60 minutes.

2 servings.

TOMATO-ENDIVE TOSS

3 cups bite-size pieces endive
2 tomatoes, cut into wedges
  Oil-and-Vinegar Dressing (page 62)
  Onion rings
  Marinated artichoke hearts, if
  desired

Toss endive, tomatoes and dressing. Garnish with onion rings and artichoke hearts.

2 servings.

MOCHA ICE-CREAM PUFFS

½ cup water
¼ cup butter or margarine
½ cup all-purpose flour
2 eggs
  Coffee ice cream
¼ cup chocolate syrup
2 teaspoons orange-flavored
  liqueur, if desired

Heat oven to 400°. In 1-quart saucepan, heat water and butter to rolling boil. Stir in flour. Stir vigorously over low heat until mixture forms a ball, about 1 minute. Remove from heat. Beat in eggs, all at one time, until smooth. Drop dough by scant ¼ cupfuls 3 inches apart onto ungreased baking sheet (makes 6 puffs). Bake until puffed and golden, about 35 minutes. Cool.

Cut off tops of 2 cream puffs. Pull out any filaments of soft dough. Fill puffs with ice cream. Mix chocolate syrup and liqueur; drizzle on cream puffs.

2 puffs—and 4 more for other times.

Note: Store the extra puffs unfilled and serve the following day or wrap in aluminum foil, label and freeze. To serve, fill with sweetened whipped cream, ice cream or pudding.

CLASSIC BEEF STROGANOFF

½ to ¾ pound beef sirloin or round
    steak, about ½ inch thick
2 tablespoons butter or margarine
¼ pound mushrooms, sliced, or
    1 can (4½ ounces) sliced
    mushrooms, drained
1 small onion, finely chopped
    (about ¼ cup)
½ cup water
1 beef bouillon cube
1 tablespoon catsup
1 small clove garlic, finely
    chopped, or ⅛ teaspoon
    instant minced garlic
½ teaspoon salt
    Poppy Seed Noodles (below)
¼ cup water
1 tablespoon flour
½ cup dairy sour cream

Cut meat into strips, 1½x½ inch. Melt butter in 8-inch skillet; cook and stir mushrooms and onion until onion is tender. Remove vegetables from skillet.

In same skillet, brown meat over medium heat. Stir in ½ cup water, the bouillon cube, catsup, garlic and salt. Reduce heat; cover and simmer 15 minutes (45 minutes if using round steak; if necessary, add small amount of water). While meat simmers, prepare Poppy Seed Noodles.

Mix ¼ cup water and the flour; stir into meat mixture. Add mushrooms and onion. Heat to boiling, stirring constantly. Boil and stir 1 minute. Stir in sour cream and heat through. Serve on the noodles.

2 servings.

Poppy Seed Noodles

Cook 4 ounces noodles (about 1½ cups) in 1 quart boiling salted water (2 teaspoons salt) until tender, about 7 minutes. Drain noodles and return to saucepan. Add 1 tablespoon butter or margarine and 1 teaspoon poppy seed and toss.

CHERRY TOMATO-BRUSSELS SPROUTS SALAD

½ package (10-ounce size) frozen
    Brussels sprouts*
¼ cup oil-and-vinegar dressing
    or Italian dressing
1 cup cherry tomatoes
2 lettuce cups

Cook Brussels sprouts as directed except —use only half the amounts of water and salt called for on package. Drain. Pour dressing on hot Brussels sprouts. Cover and refrigerate at least 3 hours.

Cut tomatoes into halves; add to Brussels sprouts and toss. Serve in lettuce cups.

2 servings.

*Leftover frozen Brussels sprouts? Serve later in the week as the vegetable at another meal. Especially good with ham, pork or turkey.

PEACHES FLAMBÉ

    Vanilla ice cream
2 tablespoons apricot jam
2 tablespoons sugar
¼ cup water
½ teaspoon lemon juice
1 can (8¾ ounces) sliced peaches,
    drained
2 tablespoons brandy

Scoop ice cream into balls; place in freezer while preparing sauce. In small chafing dish or saucepan, heat jam, sugar, water and lemon juice, stirring occasionally, until syrupy, about 5 minutes. Add peaches and heat through. Heat brandy until warm; pour on peaches and ignite immediately. Spoon peaches and sauce on ice cream.

2 servings.

Basic Know-How

Just-for-two tips on shopping,
storing and kitchen coping

What Every Kitchen for Two Needs

FOR MEASURING

Set of nested dry measuring
   cups
Liquid measuring cups
   (1-cup, 1-quart)
Measuring spoons (2 sets)
Flexible metal spatula

FOR PREPARATION

Set of mixing bowls
Wooden spoons
Metal spoons
Rubber scrapers (wide and
   narrow)
Cutting board
French knife
Bread knife
2 paring knives
Utility knife (long, narrow-
   handled)
Can opener
Bottle and jar opener
Long-handled fork
Pancake turner
Slotted spoon
Tongs
Kitchen scissors
Vegetable parer
Vegetable brush
Pastry brush
Skewers
Grater (4-sided combined
   grater and shredder)
Pepper mill
Strainer
Colander
Electric mixer
Rotary beater
Toaster
Rolling pin and cover
Pastry cloth
Pastry blender
Kitchen timer

FOR BAKING

Casseroles (20-ounce,
   1-quart, 2-quart)
Dutch oven
Individual baking dishes
   (at least 2)
6 custard cups (6-ounce
   size)
2 custard cups (10-ounce
   size)
Baking pan (8X8X2 or
   9X9X2)
Baking sheet (without sides)
2 round layer pans (9X1½)
Loaf pan (9X5X3)
Small roasting pan (with
   rack)
Muffin pan
Pie pan (8-inch)
Wire cooling rack
Pot holders
Meat thermometer

FOR TOP-OF-THE-RANGE COOKING

Covered skillets (8-inch,
   10-inch)
Covered saucepans
   (1-quart, 2-quart, 3-quart
   or Dutch oven)

SERVING PIECES

Soufflé dish
Pizza pan and pizza cutter
Chafing dish
Fondue pot and accessories
Oven-proof skillet
Ramekins
Electric hot tray
Small dessert dishes
Parfait glasses
Individual salad bowls

NICE TO HAVE

Teakettle
Coffee maker
Teapot
Double boiler
Hibachi
Griddle
Omelet pan
Tube pan
Baking pan (13X9X2)
Jelly roll pan
   (15½X10½X1)
Individual loaf pans
   (4½X2½X1½)
Electric blender
Electric skillet
Toaster-oven
Food chopper or grinder
Knife sharpener
Carving knife
Gelatin molds (individual
   and 4-cup size)
Ladle

Wire whip
Baster
Poultry shears
Mallet
Funnel
Juicer
Ice-cream scoop
Cheese slicer
Biscuit cutter (2-inch or set
   of rounds)
Melon ball cutter
Apple corer
Candy and deep fat
   thermometer
Salt and pepper set for
   range
Canister set
Cake safe
Bread box
Lettuce crisper
Utility tray
Refrigerator containers

Marketing

To be a good cook, you should be a successful shopper. After all, a menu is only as good as the foods that go into it. Here, then, are a few tips to improve your marketing know-how.

☐ Try to plan for the week ahead. Use the "specials" advertised in the newspaper as your guide to good buys.

☐ Meat will be your principal purchase. So decide on that first. Then fit the other pieces of your menu jigsaw around it.

☐ Shop with a list, but allow for flexibility. A good price on pork or fresh-picked corn is well worth a change of plans.

☐ Keep a pad in the kitchen and note any dwindling staple items—before you run out completely.

☐ Learn to list items as they're arranged in the store. Why waste time dashing back and forth?

☐ If possible, do your shopping when the store is least apt to be crowded. Avoid cart clashes, checkout-line waits, unnecessary wear and tear.

☐ Buy only what you can use— or store easily. That "two for" bargain is apt to turn into "one for" throwing out. Admittedly it's hard to hold back when potatoes are cheaper by the 10-pound sack, but resist you must, unless you're partial to sprouted Idahoes. And even the most stable of staples is better small—and more often. Nothing keeps forever!

☐ Look at the lists of have-on-hands at right and take it from there. Only by experience will you learn which foods are important for *you* to keep in stock and which ones *you* can happily live without.

STAPLES

Flour
Buttermilk baking mix
Cornmeal
Cornstarch
Sugar: granulated, brown, confectioners'
Salt and pepper
Shortening
Salad oil
Rice
Spaghetti, macaroni and noodles
Salad dressings
Vinegar
Bottled lemon juice
Baking powder
Baking soda
Cream of tartar
Vanilla
Lemon, almond, mint and sherry extracts
Worcestershire sauce
Red pepper sauce
Instant beef and chicken bouillon or bouillon cubes
Instant minced onion
Instant minced garlic or garlic powder
Parsley flakes
Mustard and catsup
Pickles and olives
Jams and jellies
Coffee and tea
Herbs and spices

FROZEN FOODS

Cubed steaks, chicken pieces, shrimp, crabmeat, fish fillets, fish sticks
Main dishes
Potatoes—French fried, patties
Vegetables and fruits
Desserts—pound cake, waffles, ice cream, sherbet, individual pies, tart shells, whipped topping
Fruit juices

CANNED FOODS

Ham, beef stew, chicken, tuna, salmon, luncheon meat, shrimp
Soups—an assortment
Fruits and vegetables
Relishes
Evaporated and condensed milk
Miscellaneous—ready-to-serve sauces, ready-to-serve puddings, fruit pie fillings, ready-to-spread frostings, toppings

PACKAGED FOODS

Soup, sauce and gravy mixes
Salad dressing mixes
Flavored gelatins
Cake mixes—several flavors
Dessert mixes and toppings
Muffin mixes
Pie crust mix
Casserole mixes—scalloped and au gratin potatoes
Rice and noodle mixes
Instant mashed potatoes
Instant nonfat dry milk
Herbed croutons
Dry bread crumbs
Soda crackers
Graham crackers and/or crumbs
Breakfast cereals
Grated Parmesan cheese

Meat

Since meat takes the biggest bite out of your food budget, it pays to get the most value and good solid nutrition for your money. That's not always easy. What appears to be a juicy steak at the meat counter may turn out to be an expensive mis-steak at your table. Inescapable conclusion: It's important to be a smart meat shopper.

How to Buy

Look before you buy. Look for flecks of fat within the lean as your clue to the meat's juiciness, flavor and tenderness. Lean meat that is bright colored, firm and fine textured denotes high quality. Look, too, for an official indication of quality.

Except for fresh pork, almost all meat is inspected and graded by the United States Department of Agriculture. The round federal inspection stamp or the USDA shield assures you that the meat is tableworthy. Grades of meat are identified on the USDA shield as "Prime," "Choice" or "Good." There *are* lesser grades, but you aren't likely to encounter them at the store. On the other hand, you won't find much "Prime" either—most of this is bought by restaurants.

A package of meat that doesn't carry either the stamp or the shield isn't necessarily a reject. Uncle Sam's seal of approval may have been marked on a part of the animal which was trimmed away. Or if you're buying something like liver or ground beef, you won't find a label at all. And in the case of veal, although it *is* graded, it's more likely to carry a label that says something like "Milk-Fed Veal," which doesn't really indicate how high up in the veal echelon that package of meat belongs.

Actually, aside from being aware of meat grades, another good way to shop for meat is to find a patient, knowledgeable meat man who will tell you what you need to know and whose wares haven't disappointed you. Even in the largest supermarket there is usually someone to guide you through the complexities of animal anatomy.

A final word on meat selection: Don't equate cost with nutrition! Budget cuts (see page 47) have as much protein value as their higher-priced cousins. Just cook them right and they'll be flavorful, delicious *and* tender. The USDA grades indicate quality, not nutritional value.

How Much to Buy

Here's an answer you may not think very helpful: "It all depends." On the face of it, that's hardly definitive. On the other hand, you can take comfort in the fact that in buying meat, there's plenty of room to move around. The "all depends" are these:

☐ How much actual *meat* (versus bone and fat) you'll get to the pound. (A pound of ground beef will obviously go quite a bit farther than a pound of spareribs will.)

☐ How old, how active and how hungry the eaters are.

☐ How much time you have for fixing and how much space for storing.

☐ How good a buy you can get. It may be worthwhile to buy a turkey or large roast and plan to use it for several meals (see pages 75–94).

How to Store

In the refrigerator: As with all perishables, the watchword is *speed.* The shorter the time lapse between the meat counter and your refrigerator, the less chance there will be of the meat losing flavor or spoiling. To be at its best, use fresh meat within 2 or 3 days, ground beef and variety meats (liver, tongue and so forth) within 24 hours. There's no harm in keeping meat in its store wrap for a day or two, but it's a good idea to loosen the ends of the package to let air reach the meat. The object of this maneuver is to dry the surface of the meat ever so slightly; this seals in the juices and also slows the growth of bacteria.

Cured and smoked meats, sausages and sandwich meats are best refrigerated in their original packages until opened. Then bundle the leftovers in a plastic bag or tight wrapping. A cured ham (in its original wrap) can be stored in the refrigerator up to 2 weeks. Most canned hams should be

HOW MUCH TO BUY?

BONELESS CUTS	¼ to ⅓ lb.
(such as ground meat, stew meat, tenderloin)	per serving
BONELESS ROASTS	⅓ to ½ lb.
(such as rolled beef, pork shoulder, beef tip)	per serving
MEDIUM BONE IN	½ to ¾ lb.
(such as pot roast, country-style ribs)	per serving
LARGE BONE IN	¾ to 1 lb.
(such as shanks, short ribs, spareribs)	per serving

stored in the refrigerator. If un-opened, they can be kept safely up to 6 months.

Leftover cooked meat? Same treatment. Cool quickly; cover and refrigerate promptly. Finish up in 1 or 2 days...or wrap tightly and freeze; the time limits are:
☐ Plain—1 month
☐ With broth or gravy—6 months

In the freezer: If you plan to freeze meat, do it as soon after shopping as possible — because the quality you put in is the quality you'll take out.

Just about all meats freeze well and maintain their quality if wrapped properly, frozen quickly and stored at a temperature of 0° or below. Be sure to use a moisture-vapor-proof wrap such as heavy-duty aluminum foil, heavily waxed freezer paper or specially laminated paper. Wrap the meat tightly—the intent here is to eliminate as much air as possible from within the package. An improperly wrapped package can spell disaster. If air gets in, it will draw moisture from the meat and the meat will become dry, less flavorful and show indications of freezer burn (discoloration).

Meat bought already frozen can go from the store's freezer to yours "as is," but don't forget to mark it with the date. (Make sure the meat cut and its weight are also noted.) You can also freeze *fresh* meat in the transparent wrap it comes in—providing you plan to use it within a week or two. For longer storage, tuck the original package into a heavyweight plastic bag, or overwrap with any sturdy freezer material. Press all the air out of the package before sealing.

To conserve freezer space

HOW LONG TO STORE?
(For best quality, consider these periods maximum.)

	DAYS In Refrigerator (35 to 40°F.)	MONTHS In Freezer (0° F.)
Steaks (beef)	3 to 5	8 to 12
Chops (lamb and pork)	3 to 5	3 to 4
Ground Meats	1 to 2	2 to 3
Stew Meats	1 to 2	2 to 3
Roasts (beef and lamb)	3 to 5	8 to 12
Roasts (pork)	3 to 5	4 to 8
Liver and Variety Meats	1 to 2	3 to 4
Corned Brisket	7	½
Frankfurters	7	½
Bacon	7	1
Sausage (pork)	1 to 2	1 to 2
Ham (half)	3 to 5	1 to 2
Ham (slices)	3	1 to 2
Ham (canned)	6 months	Don't freeze
Luncheon Meats	3 to 5	Don't freeze
Sausage (smoked)	7	Don't freeze
Sausage (dry and semidry)	14 to 21	Don't freeze

and save time later, you may want to get your meat ready for the pan before freezing. Trim off excess fat; divide meat into portions; form ground beef into patties; separate chops, small steaks and patties with a double thickness of aluminum foil or waxed paper. Such do-aheads will make life easier for you at the thawing end. The only thing you *don't* want to do is season meat beforehand, as salt shortens freezer life.

Reminder: Label and date—not only with the date you put the package *in* but also with the "expiration date," by which time you should check it *out.* Follow the chart above for an idea of how long specific meats can be stored before quality begins to go noticeably downhill. Note that these maximum times apply *only* if your freezer stays at 0° or colder. If your sole freezer space is located over the refrigerator compartment and has no separate door, you shouldn't count on keeping

foods frozen for longer than a week: A constant temperature of 0° just isn't possible under those conditions.

To thaw: First know that frozen meat can be cooked satisfactorily while still in its frozen state (with the exception of thick pork steaks and pork roasts, which must be at least partially thawed in order to insure thorough cooking). But if you do choose to thaw your meat before cooking, a few easy dos and don'ts will help to keep it in the pink of condition.

Slow-thaw method—If possible, allow meat to thaw, still freezer-wrapped, in the refrigerator. For a 3- to 5-pound roast, it will take 3 to 5 hours per pound. For a 1-inch steak, count on approximately 12 to 14 hours.

Fast-thaw method—Although there is some chance of spoilage, meat *can* be thawed at room temperature. Keep wrapped. For small roasts, allow 1 to 2 hours per pound. For a 1-inch steak, allow 2 to 4 hours. Cook the meat while it's still chilled.

Fastest-thaw method—Meat that is destined to be braised or pot roasted can be thawed by covering the sealed package with cold water. Then there's the...

No-thaw method—You can start to cook almost any cut of meat while it's still frozen; just add extra cooking time.

Cooking Frozen Meat

Roasts: A small roast will take from one third to half again as long to cook as one that has been thawed. The actual additional time depends on the thickness. Let the roast cook about an hour before inserting the meat thermometer.

Steaks, chops, burgers: These will take from one fourth to half again as long to cook as meat that has been thawed. To broil —Keep the meat farther away from the heat source than you do when it's thawed; this will prevent it from being charred on the outside and raw in the center. (Add an additional distance of 2 inches for any cut thicker than ¾ inch.) To panbroil—Be sure to heat the skillet before adding the meat, and brown it quickly. The idea is to beat the thaw to the draw. If the surface starts to thaw *before* it's browned, chances are it won't brown well at all. Once the meat is browned, turn down the heat to let it cook to the desired degree of doneness.

A word about refreezing: Meat, once thawed, can be refrozen *only* if some ice crystals remain. *But* don't expect meat to be as flavorful or juicy if it's refrozen, as some of the good juices will have been lost in the original thaw-out.

Fish

For a change-of-pace, highly nutritious meal that can be as kindly in cost as it is in calories, fish is your dish. What's more, fish is quick to fix, and most varieties come in handy serving-size portions.

Fresh Fish

When you shop for a whole fish, look for bright, clear, bulging eyes; firm flesh that springs back when pressed; reddish-pink gills; shiny, bright-colored scales, close to the skin. All fresh fish should *smell* fresh and not too strong. For each serving, you'll need:

☐ Whole—¾ to 1 pound
☐ Steaks—½ pound
☐ Fillets—⅓ to ½ pound

To store in refrigerator: Wrap in moisture-proof airtight material, or place in a tightly covered container and refrigerate pronto! (Only the coldest section of your refrigerator will do.) If you don't plan to use the fish in a day or two, freeze it.

To freeze: Assuming whole fish has been cleaned (and scaled if necessary), wash under running cold water, drain, gently pat dry and wrap tightly in a moisture-vapor-proof wrap such as heavy foil, freezer paper or plastic wrap.

Steaks and fillets should be separated by a double thickness of foil or waxed paper and then tightly wrapped.

Label and date all packages.

To thaw: Place still-wrapped frozen fish in the refrigerator (allow about 8 hours to thaw a 1-pound package). For speedier thawing, leave fish in its freezer wrap and cover with cold water, changing the water frequently (a 1-pound package

will thaw in about 2 hours). Fillets and steaks can be cooked without thawing—but give them extra cooking time.

Frozen Fish

Frozen fish comes in an ever-increasing variety of portions in addition to steaks and fillets —squares, rounds, sticks, rectangles—some breaded, some not, some precooked, some ready for cooking. Aside from relying on the package for directions, there are just a few general "need to knows":

☐ ⅓ to ½ pound serves one.
☐ Fish portions and sticks should go directly from freezer to pan; don't thaw them first. If they do thaw, use immediately; don't refreeze.
☐ Storage limit—6 months.

Shellfish

Although usually considered a luxury, in the small quantities needed for two, shellfish is often no more costly than meat. Especially since it takes so well to being stretched with sauces, pasta or rice. Figure an average serving about like this:

☐ Shrimp—5 to 7 large (about 15 per pound) or 10 to 15 medium (about 28 per pound)
☐ Lobster tails—1 large or 2 small
☐ Lobster meat—¼ pound
☐ Crabmeat—¼ pound
☐ Scallops—⅓ to ½ pound
☐ Oysters, clams—½ pint shucked or 6 in the shell

Be sure the shells of oysters and clams are tightly closed. Shrimp and scallops should have a clean, fresh smell; whole lobsters should be alive (or cooked).

Refrigerate all shellfish promptly and use as soon as possible—within 1 day. Observe the same guidelines for shellfish bought frozen as for other fish.

Poultry

The pleasures of poultry are many, and not the least of these is economy. But that's just for starters. Count also among its attributes...

☐ Variety—dozens of ways to buy it.

☐ Versatility—hundreds of ways to fix it.

☐ Availability—no more just the Sunday chicken and the Thanksgiving turkey; you can enjoy poultry any day and any season.

How to Buy

Broiler-fryer chicken: About 1½ to 3 pounds; allow ½ to 1 pound per person. Comes fresh or frozen and either ready-to-cook or cooked and ready to reheat. Buy whole, halved, quartered or cut into serving pieces. Also packaged in parts: drumsticks, breasts, thighs, wings, livers, gizzards. Even though you may pay a little more per pound, chicken parts can be a thrifty no-waste buy for two. Besides, you can start with your favorite pieces! The broiler-fryer is really an all-purpose chicken; suitable preparation methods include not only broiling and frying but also roasting and stewing. For casseroles and dishes like creamed chicken, remember that a 2½-pound broiler-fryer yields approximately 2 cups cut-up cooked chicken.

Roaster chicken: Weighing 3½ to 5 pounds, this is a little larger and older than the broiler-fryer. It is the best choice for roasting but can also be used for stewing.

Rock Cornish hen: About 1 to 1½ pounds. The smaller size of this minimember of the chicken family is just right for a single serving; the larger size is fine for two. Usually comes frozen. Can be roasted stuffed or unstuffed, or can be split and broiled.

Duckling: About 3½ to 5 pounds will be fine for two. A special treat for dark-meat lovers, for unlike chicken and turkey, even the breast is dark. Comes whole, fresh or frozen. Roast whole, stuffed or unstuffed, or cut up for braising or baking.

Turkey: A 4- to 9-pound fryer-roaster is the best size for two (allow ½ to 1 pound per person). Comes whole, fresh or frozen; frozen turkeys may be stuffed or unstuffed. Also available halved, quartered, cut into serving pieces or by the part (drumsticks, thighs, wings and occasionally breasts). Roast; cut-up fryer-roaster can also be broiled, panfried, braised or barbecued.

Boneless turkey roll: About 2 to 5 pounds. Comes frozen, with all white meat or a combination of white and dark meat. Available with or without gravy.

Ground turkey: Sold by the pound, like ground meats (½ pound serves two). Low in fat and low in calories, thrifty, tasty ground turkey is almost as versatile as hamburger. Follow the same storing and freezing directions as for ground beef (see page 115).

How to Store

In the refrigerator: Quick—to the refrigerator . . . and always where it's coldest! Keep loosely covered or in its transparent store wrap. Use within 1 to 2 days.

In the freezer: For short-term storage (up to 2 weeks), the transparent store wrap does nicely for prepackaged poultry. If you plan to freeze longer, overwrap the store package with a moisture-vapor-proof wrap (heavy-duty foil, plastic wrap or a plastic bag). Or wash, pat dry and wrap snugly in your favorite freezer material. (Giblets should be frozen separately.) And don't forget to label and date packages. Storage limit at 0° or lower:

☐ Poultry—6 months
☐ Giblets—6 months

To thaw: Slowly, slowly is the best way. Which means thaw in the refrigerator rather than on the kitchen counter. Allow the following times:

☐ Chicken parts—4 to 9 hours
☐ Whole chicken—12 hours
☐ Rock Cornish hen—9 to 12 hours
☐ Turkey parts—9 to 12 hours
☐ 4- to 9-pound turkey—1 to 2 days

In a hurry? Cover frozen poultry, still tightly wrapped, with cold water, changing the water occasionally. A whole chicken will thaw in 1 to 2 hours; a whole turkey in 3 to 4 hours.

Leftover cooked poultry? Store well-wrapped in the refrigerator for 1 to 2 days *(always package any stuffing separately)*. Freezer times:

☐ Plain—1 month
☐ With broth or gravy—6 months

Freezing tips: Is poultry frozen beyond the recommended time limits still safe? If properly stored, yes. But don't expect the taste or texture to be as good. Can poultry be refrozen once it's thawed? Better not! Although there is this exception: Frozen, uncooked poultry can be thawed and *cooked* and the leftovers then frozen for another time.

Some Good Meat Choices for Two

LOOK FOR THESE CUTS	COOK THEM PROPERLY

BEEF

Ground: Use in patties, loaves or main-dish casseroles. Regular (25 to 30% fat, some shrinkage), Lean (20 to 25% fat, less shrinkage), Extra Lean (15 to 20% fat, very little shrinkage). — Broil. Panbroil. Panfry. (Bake loaves and casseroles.)

Short Ribs: Cut from the ends of chuck or rib roasts. — Braise or cook in liquid.

Stew Meat: Cut from chuck, tip, short plate and foreshank. Usually cut into 1-inch pieces; should contain small amount of fat. — Braise or cook in liquid.

Chuck Roast: Choose arm (round bone), blade or boneless roasts; can be cut up and cooked in small quantities. — Braise.

Chuck Steak: Available either boneless or with a round or blade bone. Economical. — Braise. Can be broiled if of high quality or if tenderized.

Top Loin Steak: Small steak in the short loin; has no tenderloin. Just the right size for individual servings. — Broil. (Panbroil if less than ¾ inch thick.)

Cubed Steak: Also called Minute Steak. Machine-cubed. — Panfry.

Flank Steak: Also called London Broil. Long, coarse fibers; sometimes scored in diamonds for tenderness. — Braise. Can be broiled if of high quality and marinated.

Porterhouse Steak: Has a section of tenderloin and a section of top loin steak divided by a T-shaped bone. Tenderloin can be removed and served separately as Filet Mignon. — Broil. (Panbroil if less than ¾ inch thick.)

Rib Steak: Cut from the rib section—actually this is a slice of rib roast, with bone or boneless. — Broil. (Panbroil if less than ¾ inch thick.)

Rib Eye Steak: Also called Delmonico Steak. Cut from the eye of beef rib. Boneless, has little fat, very tender. — Broil. (Panbroil if less than ¾ inch thick.)

Round Steak: The top round is sometimes more tender than the bottom round. (Large steaks can be cut into meal-size portions.) Economical because of very little waste. — Braise. Can be broiled if of high quality or if tenderized.

Sirloin Steak: Bone in or boneless; the amount of bone varies from steak to steak. Less expensive than most steaks, it's a good choice for two. — Broil. (Panbroil if less than ¾ inch thick.)

T-Bone Steak: Similar to porterhouse but smaller, with a smaller tenderloin portion. — Broil. (Panbroil if less than ¾ inch thick.)

Tenderloin Steak: Better known as Filet Mignon. Boneless, very little fat, tenderest of all steaks; expensive. — Broil.

Broiling

For tender steaks and chops, sliced ham, bacon, ground meat, baby beef liver. (Steaks and chops should be at least ¾ inch thick.)
1. Set oven to broil and/or 550°.
2. Broil with meat surface 2 to 5 inches (depending on thickness) from heat until brown. Season only after browning.
3. Turn and broil to desired degree of doneness. Season.

Panbroiling

For tender steaks and chops, sliced ham, bacon, ground meat. (All cuts should be thin—no more than 1 inch thick.)
1. Place meat in heavy skillet. (For very lean meat cuts, brush skillet with shortening.)
2. Do not add fat or water. Do not cover.
3. Cook slowly. Turn occasionally to brown and cook meat evenly. Pour off fat from skillet as it accumulates.
4. Cook until done. Season.

Panfrying

For thin, tender steaks and chops, cutlets, ground meat, liver and pieces which have been tenderized by scoring, cubing or grinding.
1. Brown on both sides in small amount of fat. (Fat is not needed in a pan with non-stick coating.)
2. Season with salt and pepper.
3. Do not cover.
4. Cook over medium heat, turning occasionally, until done.

Some Good Meat Choices for Two

LOOK FOR THESE CUTS	COOK THEM PROPERLY

PORK

Bacon: The cured and smoked side of pork. — Broil. Panbroil. Panfry.

Canadian-style Bacon: A cured and smoked boneless loin of pork, leaner than regular bacon. — Roast (bake). Broil. Panbroil. Panfry.

Chops: Blade, rib, loin and sirloin chops are available, cut thick or thin. Extra-thin chops cook quickly and are a time-saver. — Roast (bake). Broil. Panbroil. Braise.

Ham Slice: Cut from smoked ham. Available in a variety of thicknesses. — Roast (bake). Broil. Panbroil. Panfry.

Canned Ham: The 1½-pound size is good for two. Follow directions on can. — Roast (bake).

Ribs: (Spareribs, back ribs and country-style ribs.) Proportion of meat to fat to bone varies considerably; prices vary accordingly. — Roast (bake). Braise.

Sausages: Available in great variety—frankfurters, Polish sausages, bratwurst, knackwurst, etc. — Roast (bake). Broil. Panbroil. Panfry.

Smoked Chops: Only the loin cut is available. — Broil. Roast (bake).

Smoked Shoulder Roll: Boneless. Like Canadian-style bacon, but has more fat distributed throughout the meat. Economical. A 1- to 2-pound size is good for two. Follow package directions or use like ham. — Roast (bake). Cook in liquid. Broil. Panbroil. Panfry.

Steak: Arm or blade cuts are available. A good buy. — Braise. Panfry.

Tenderloin: Boneless; whole, sliced or flattened. Very tender. Frozen tenderloins are good for two; follow package directions. — Roast (bake). Panfry. Braise.

LAMB

Chops: Shoulder, rib, loin and sirloin chops are available. (Shoulder chops are the most economical.) — Broil. Panbroil.

Ground: Made from the less tender cuts. Shape into meat loaf or patties. — Roast (bake). Broil. Panbroil. Panfry.

Shanks: Foreshanks and hindshanks are available. A 1-pound shank is just right for one person. — Braise. Cook in liquid.

VEAL

Chops: Rib, loin and sirloin chops are available. — Braise. Panfry.

Cutlets: Cut from round steak. — Braise. Panfry.

Roasting	Braising	Cooking in Liquid
For large, tender cuts of beef, veal, pork and lamb.	For less tender meat cuts (pot roasts, round steak, short ribs), stew meat and some tender cuts (pork chops and cutlets).	For large, less tender meat cuts (beef corned brisket, pork hocks, lamb shanks) and stew meat.
1. Place fat side up on rack in shallow roasting pan.	**1.** Brown on all sides in heavy pan, skillet or Dutch oven, adding fat if necessary.	**1.** Brown meat on all sides in own fat or other fat, if desired, in heavy pan, skillet or Dutch oven.
2. Insert meat thermometer so it is centered in thickest part, not resting in fat or on bone.	**2.** Season with salt and pepper.	**2.** Cover meat with liquid.
3. Do not add water. Do not cover.	**3.** Add small amount of liquid if necessary.	**3.** Season; cover and simmer until tender.
4. Roast at 325° until done. (See roasting charts for time, temperature and degree of doneness.)	**4.** Cover tightly. Simmer on top of range or in 300 to 325° oven until meat is tender.	**4.** Add vegetables just long enough before serving to cook them through.

Some Good Vegetable Choices for Two

WHAT TO BUY	WHAT TO LOOK FOR	HOW TO STORE
Artichokes (1 per person)	Thick, green, fresh-looking leaves on plump, compact, globular heads; avoid spreading leaves.	Store in refrigerator, either in crisper or plastic bag. Will keep up to 4 days.
Asparagus (1 bunch—½ to ¾ pound)	Smooth, round spears with a fresh appearance. Tips should be closed and compact.	Store in refrigerator, either in crisper or plastic bag. Will keep up to 2 days.
Cabbage (1 small head—2 cups shredded)	A firm head, with fresh, well-colored outer leaves.	Store in refrigerator, either in crisper or plastic bag. Will keep up to 4 weeks.
Carrots (1 bunch—5 or 6 medium)	Smooth, firm, well shaped; a good orange color.	Store in refrigerator, either in crisper or plastic bag. Will keep up to 2 weeks.
Cauliflower (1 small head or ½ large head)	Clean, compact, white to creamy-white curds (the edible white portion); good green leaves.	Store in refrigerator, either in crisper or plastic bag. Will keep up to 5 days.
Celery (1 small bunch)	Crisp, solid stalks with a glossy surface. Avoid bunches with discoloration of center stalks.	Store in refrigerator, either in crisper or plastic bag. Will keep up to 8 days.
Corn on the Cob (About 4 ears)	Green, fresh-looking husks. The silk at the husk opening should be dark brown, and the ears should be well covered with plump kernels.	For best eating quality, cook as soon as possible after picking. If you must store corn, refrigerate unhusked and uncovered. Will keep up to 2 days.
Cucumber (1 medium)	Firm, good green color, not too large in diameter. Avoid cucumbers that look withered or shriveled.	Store in refrigerator, either in crisper or plastic bag. Will keep up to 2 weeks.
Eggplant (1 small—½ to ¾ pound)	Firm, heavy, with smooth skin of an even dark purple color. Avoid eggplants that are soft, shriveled or marked with dark brown spots.	Store in refrigerator, in crisper. Will keep up to 2 weeks.
Lettuce (1 medium head lettuce yields about 6 cups bite-size pieces)	Fresh, unwilted greens. Head lettuce should be medium firm and of medium size; outer leaves, varying from light to dark green, should be free of rust marks. Select well-rounded heads of Boston, heavy for their size, with tender leaves ranging from white to medium green. Look for fairly compact heads of romaine; the long green outer leaves should be stiff, with white to light green ribs.	Store as soon as possible in refrigerator, either in crisper or plastic bag. Before storing, wash lettuce under running cold water; drain or pat dry *thoroughly*. Head and romaine lettuce can be kept up to 1 week, other varieties for a shorter time.
Mushrooms (¼ to ½ pound)	Firm caps of white or creamy color, depending on the species. Avoid mushrooms with flat, open caps or cracked stems.	Store in refrigerator (spread on shallow pan or tray; cover with damp cloth). Will keep up to 4 days. Before using, wipe with damp cloth or rinse and wipe dry.

Some Good Vegetable Choices for Two

WHAT TO BUY	WHAT TO LOOK FOR	HOW TO STORE
Onions (½ pound)	Hard, firm globes; paper-thin outer skins. (Yellow and white globe onions are the most common and are primarily used for cooking. Bermuda-type onions have a mild flavor and are ideal for slicing, eating [raw] and cooking. Spanish onions are easy to slice and great in salads.)	Store in a cool, dry, well ventilated place. Onions will keep for 2 weeks at room temperature, longer at a temperature of 45 to 50°. Do not refrigerate.
Parsley (1 bunch)	Crisp, bright, deep green leaves.	Store in refrigerator. Before storing, wash under running cold water, then shake to remove excess moisture. Place in jar and cover.
Peppers (Sweet Bell) (1 medium)	Relatively heavy in weight, with firm, well-shaped, thick "walls." Color should be a medium to dark green.	Store in refrigerator, either in crisper or plastic bag. Will keep up to 5 days.
Potatoes (2 medium potatoes or ¾ pound new potatoes)	Evenly shaped, mature, of medium size, firm and without cuts, blemishes, green discoloration or sprouts. General-purpose potatoes—like Russet Burbank, Cherokee, Kennebec—are mealy and excellent for baking and mashing. New potatoes should be well shaped, firm, free from blemishes and sunburn; they are ideal boiled and in salads.	Store at room temperature, in a place with good ventilation. Will keep up to 2 weeks—longer at 45 to 50° temperature. Do not refrigerate. New potatoes will keep up to 4 days—longer at 45 to 50° temperature.
Spinach (1 pound of fresh spinach, cooked)	Crisp, dark green leaves; avoid leaves that are crushed or wilted.	Store in refrigerator. Will keep up to 3 days. Before using, remove imperfect leaves and root ends. Wash just before using if spinach is to be cooked. For salads, wash leaves, drain and dry.
Squash (1 medium acorn squash or 2 to 4 zucchini)	Tough-skinned acorn squash, hard and heavy for its size; avoid sunken or moldy spots and skin punctures. Zucchini should be firm and well formed with tender, glossy skins.	*Acorn squash:* Store at room temperature; will keep up to 2 weeks—longer at 60° temperature. Do not refrigerate. *Zucchini:* Store in refrigerator, either in crisper or plastic bag. Will keep up to 5 days.
Sweet Potatoes (2 medium)	Smooth, plump, dry; uniform in shape and color.	Store at room temperature, with good ventilation. Will keep up to 2 weeks—longer at 60° temperature. Do not refrigerate.
Tomatoes (1 pound)	Well formed, smooth, well ripened and reasonably free of blemishes.	Store in refrigerator, in crisper. Will keep up to 1 week. (If necessary, keep at room temperature until ripe.)

Some Good Fruit Choices for Two

WHAT TO BUY	WHAT TO LOOK FOR	HOW TO STORE
Apples (about 3 medium in 1 pound)	Firm, crisp, with good color. Avoid apples that are bruised or have a shriveled appearance. For eating, Delicious, McIntosh, Winesap and Northern Spy are among the best. For cooking, Baldwin, Greening and Winesap are good choices.	Store in a cool, dry place or in refrigerator. Will keep up to 2 weeks.
Avocados (1 is enough for 2 servings)	Slightly soft—it should yield to gentle pressure. Avoid avocados with sunken spots or broken surfaces.	Store at room temperature until soft to the touch. When ripe, place in warmest section of refrigerator. Will keep up to 5 days.
Bananas (about 3 medium in 1 pound)	Firm fruit, fully ripened or green. A ripened banana should have a uniform yellow color and brown specks.	Store at room temperature until ripe—bananas ripen quickly. Never refrigerate unless fully ripened.
Cantaloupe (½ to 1 medium per person)	Skin of yellowish-gray or pale yellow color, with a texture like coarse, thick netting. Should have a pleasant cantaloupe odor.	Store in refrigerator in a plastic bag—the bag helps to confine the odor. Will keep up to 8 days. (If necessary, keep at room temperature until ripe.)
Grapefruit (1 is enough for 2 servings)	Firm, smoothly textured, well shaped, heavy for its size. Thin-skinned grapefruit are very juicy. Avoid grapefruit with pointed stem ends or rough, wrinkled skins.	Store in refrigerator or in a cool place. Will keep 2 weeks or longer.
Grapes (½ to 1 pound)	Well colored, plump; firmly attached to the stem.	Store unwashed and uncovered in refrigerator. Will keep up to 5 days.
Oranges (2 to 3 oranges yield 1 cup of juice)	Firm, heavy for their size. Navel oranges (seedless) are best for slices and sections; Valencia oranges are preferred for juice.	Store uncovered in refrigerator or in a cool place. Will keep 2 weeks or longer.
Peaches (about 3 medium in 1 pound)	Fairly firm or just a trifle soft. The skin color between the red areas should be yellow or creamy.	Store in refrigerator, in crisper. Will keep up to 1 week. (If necessary, keep at room temperature until ripe.)
Pears (about 3 medium in 1 pound)	For Bartletts, look for a pale yellow to rich yellow color; for D'Anjou or Comice, light green to yellowish green; for Bosc, greenish yellow to brownish yellow. All varieties should be firm.	Store in refrigerator, in crisper. (If necessary, keep at room temperature until ripe.)
Pineapple (1 is enough for 2 servings)	Heavy for its size, slightly soft, golden in color. The fruit should have a fragrant pineapple odor. Avoid fruit with signs of decay at the base or on sides.	Store in refrigerator or in a cool place. Will keep up to 2 days. Wrap the pineapple in a plastic bag—the bag helps to keep the fragrance confined to the pineapple.
Strawberries (1 pint)	Firm berries of a bright, lustrous color; caps and stems should be firmly attached.	Store unwashed and uncovered in refrigerator. Will keep up to 2 days.

How Much Is Enough?

FOOD	IF YOU HAVE...	YOU'LL GET...
Apple	1 medium	1 cup chopped
Banana	1 to 2 medium	1 cup sliced
	3 medium	1 cup mashed
Beans, dried (small)	8 ounces	3 cups cooked
Butter or margarine	1 pound	2 cups
	¼ pound or 1 stick	½ cup
Cabbage	¼ pound	1 cup shredded
Carrots	1 to 2 medium	1 cup shredded
	2 to 3 medium	1 cup thinly sliced
Celery	2 medium stalks	1 cup sliced
Cheese		
Cheddar or American	4 ounces	1 cup shredded
cottage	8 ounces	1 cup
cream	3-ounce package	6 tablespoons
	8-ounce package	1 cup (16 tablespoons)
Chicken (cooked)	2½-pound broiler-fryer	2 cups diced
Chocolate		
chips	6-ounce package	1 cup
unsweetened	8-ounce package	8 squares (1 ounce each)
Cereal (flakes)	3 cups	1 cup crushed
Crackers		
graham	12 squares	1 cup fine crumbs
soda	20 squares	1 cup coarse crumbs
Cream		
sour	8 ounces	1 cup
whipping	1 cup (½ pint)	2 cups whipped
Flour		
all-purpose	1 pound	3½ cups
cake	1 pound	4 cups
Green pepper	1 medium	1 cup chopped
Lemon		
juice	1 medium	2 to 3 tablespoons
peel	1 medium	1½ teaspoons grated
Macaroni (elbow)	½ of 8-ounce package	2 cups cooked
Meat (cooked)	6 to 7 ounces	1 cup julienne strips
Milk (evaporated)	1 can (6 ounces)	⅔ cup
	1 can (14½ ounces)	1⅔ cups
Noodles (regular)	4 ounces	2 cups cooked
Nuts	4 ounces (shelled)	1 cup chopped
Onions	1 medium	½ cup chopped
Rice		
brown	½ cup (uncooked)	1¾ to 2 cups cooked
parboiled (converted)	½ cup (uncooked)	1½ to 1¾ cups cooked
precooked (instant)	1 cup (uncooked)	1 to 2 cups cooked
regular white	½ cup (uncooked)	1½ cups cooked
wild	½ cup (uncooked)	1½ cups cooked
Strawberries	1 pint	2 cups sliced
Sugar		
brown (firmly packed)	1 pound	2¼ cups
confectioners' (unsifted)	1 pound	4 cups
granulated	1 pound	2¼ cups